HAYS AND GOTT FAMILIES

HERITAGE BOOKS
AN IMPRINT OF HERITAGE BOOKS, INC.

Books, CDs, and more—Worldwide

For our listing of thousands of titles see our website
at
www.HeritageBooks.com

Published 2007 by
HERITAGE BOOKS, INC.
Publishing Division
65 East Main Street
Westminster, Maryland 21157-5026

International Standard Book Number: 978-0-7884-2033-7

Our Maryland Heritage

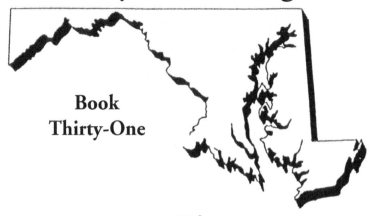

Book Thirty-One

The

Hays and Gott Families

William N. Hurley, Jr.

HERITAGE BOOKS
2007

ALSO BY W. N. HURLEY, JR.

Available from the publisher: Heritage Books, Inc.

1900 Census of Montgomery County, Maryland
Winner of the 2001 Norris Harris Prize, Maryland Historical Society
"Best compilation of genealogical source records of Maryland"

Our Maryland Heritage Series:

INTRODUCTION

This is the Thirty-first in our series of families having their origins in Maryland, with descendants now found in all parts of the United States. This study of the Hays and Gott families has been limited somewhat to those members of the families having their origins primarily in Frederick and Montgomery Counties, Maryland, although others will be mentioned as they are found elsewhere.

As colonists continued to arrive, seven original counties were formed in Maryland under the Colonial Governor: Anne Arundel; Charles; Kent; Somerset; St. Mary's; Calvert; and Talbot. As settlers moved steadily westward, and took up new lands, it was necessary to form new centers of government to serve them and, over time, sixteen new counties were formed from the original seven, as well as the City of Baltimore. The researcher must be familiar with this formation, in order to know the sources of information for any given time-frame. The following tabulation demonstrates the formation of each of the counties of Maryland:

Formation of the Counties of Maryland

Name of County	Formed	Source County or Counties
Allegany	1789	Washington
Anne Arundel	1650	Original County
Baltimore	1660	Anne Arundel
Calvert	1654	Original County
Caroline	1773	Dorchester & Queen Anne's
Carroll	1837	Baltimore & Frederick
Cecil	1674	Baltimore & Kent
Charles	1658	Original County
Dorchester	1669	Somerset & Talbot
Frederick	1748	Prince George's & Baltimore
Garrett	1872	Allegany
Harford	1773	Baltimore

Howard	1851	Anne Arundel
Kent	1642	Original County
Montgomery	1776	Frederick
Prince George's	1695	Calvert & Charles
Queen Anne's	1706	Dorchester, Kent & Talbot
Somerset	1666	Original County
St. Mary's	1637	Original County
Talbot	1662	Original County
Washington	1776	Frederick
Wicomico	1867	Somerset & Worcester
Worcester	1742	Somerset

A WORD OF CAUTION

The data contained in this report is not intended to be an all-inclusive genealogy of the families under study. It was prepared from information found in a variety of sources, including records found at the library of the Montgomery County Historical Society, such as family files, census returns, church and cemetery records, obituary collections, and the published books and abstracts held by the library in their research collection. We have not confirmed all of the data by personal examination of contemporary records, and can not, therefore, vouch for its accuracy in all cases. Others are, of course, just as prone to making mistakes as we are, but the information reported is as accurate as we could make it from the records studied.

The Hays and Gott families are among the major ones found in the records of old Medley District in upper Montgomery County, and in the Monocacy Cemetery at Beallsville. They intermarried in several generations with members of the prominent families of All-nutt, White, Darby, Chiswell and others. Volumes of research have been prepared on these important families, especially the Allnutt, Darby and Chiswell families, and are to be found in the library of the Montgomery County Historical Society in Rockville. We will not attempt here to reproduce those very extensive genealogies, and refer the reader there for further information.

Simply as an example of the extent of the intermarriages among these old families, examine the family of Richard **Gott**, born October 24, 1807. His wife was Mary Elizabeth **Trundle**. Eldest daughter Mary Ellen married Thomas E. **White**. Second daughter Sarah Elizabeth married Elijah Viers **White**. Fourth daughter Jane Sabelle married Robert **Dade**. Fifth daughter Ann Virginia married Benjamin J. **Jones**. Son John Spinks Gott married Florence Elizabeth **Hays**. And so it went throughout the generations.

Additionally, and importantly, in the Maryland Genealogical Society Bulletins, Volume 33, Number 2, Spring of 1992, contains a report by Ernest C. Allnutt, Jr. of Baltimore, running to thirty pages, reporting on one of the lines of descent from Richard Gott, the immigrant, through six generations. It is filled with source data and references, discussions of the lives of the various family members, historical perspectives and, of course, detailed genealogical information relative to the lineage discussed. It is highly recommended for further review.

We recognize that it is virtually impossible to report such an extensive amount of data without an error creeping in some place. Occasionally, we may have reported a date of birth, which is in reality the date of christening, or vice versa. Some reported dates of marriage are probably the date a license was issued, as reported in the public records, but should be reasonably close. In some cases, we will report dates as approximate, but they should lead you to the general time frame, so that you may distinguish between individuals with the same name. Throughout the text, I have used terms which should caution the reader: such as, apparently; may have been; reportedly; about; possibly; could be; and similar terminology, to indicate that the information given has either not been verified by extant contemporary records, or appears to fit a given set of circumstances which, of themselves, are believed to be correct.

Our goal has been to gather all of the available material into one convenient package, which should be accurate enough to provide the casual reader with an insight into their family history. The serious researcher should verify the material with independent research. Good luck, and please forgive our occasional error.

AND A WORD OF APPRECIATION

As mentioned in the Introduction, this is the thirty-first volume in our series titled generally *Our Maryland Heritage*. None of the books in the series could have been produced without assistance from a number of people; too many to list here individually.

Most importantly, I want to thank Jane Sween, the now retired librarian of the Montgomery County Historical Society, and the volunteers who worked with her. Jane has untiringly assisted me with research of the files of the library, with the knowledge that only she possesses. It is also Jane who has guided me toward each new family for study, suggesting which might be the most important for the next effort. Jane is unquestionably the most valuable resource that can be found in the library, and without her, much of the available information would be difficult, if not impossible, to find.

Beyond that, there has been a great personal satisfaction derived from our conversations, and our mutual interest.

In addition to Jane, much encouragement and guidance has been given me by Pat Anderson, a recognized author and genealogist in her own right, who served as Jane's assistant for many years, and was appointed librarian following Jane's retirement, and by other volunteers at the Historical Society Library. For that, I will always be grateful.

As a result of their continued assistance, from the outset the commitment was made that with publication of each of the books in the series, all royalties derived are paid directly to the account of the Montgomery County Historical Society, for use of the library.

CONTENTS

Order of Presentation

Arrangement of the Principal Chapters

Thomas Hays
1678-1747
Chapter 1
*

*

William Hays, Sr.
died c.1791
*

*

Leonard Hays
1759-1822
Chapter 2
*

*

Samuel Simmons Hays
1787-
*

*

* * * * * * * * *
*   *

Elizabeth Eleanoy Hays	John H. T. Hays
1818-1855	1813-
Chapter 3	*
	Florence Elizabeth Hays
	1849-
	married
	John Spinks Gott

x

    a.   Charles Hays, 3rd. He is perhaps the same who was married January 12, 1802 in Frederick County to Sarah Hilton; and listed in the 1820 census with as many as eight sons and two daughters.

    b.   Thomas Hays.

    c.   Eleanor Hays, married to Joseph Kibby under license dated August 25, 1795

    d.   Martha Hays.

    e.   Anne Rawlings Hays.

    f.   Lily Rawlings Hays.

4.   Levi Hays, born October 1, 1752 in Montgomery County, died October 10, 1825 in Pickaway County, Ohio. Married December 9, 1779 Montgomery County, Maryland to Eleanor Harris, born there c.1752, died April 7, 1814 in Pickaway County, Ohio. She was a daughter of Joseph Harris. Levi and Eleanor had children, born in Montgomery County before the move to Ohio:

    a.   Joseph Hays, born c.1781, died August, 1852. Married October 11, 1816 to Sarah Hill.

    b.   Norris Harris Hays, born c.1784, died June 24, 1850. Married September 21, 1826 to Sarah Hurst, born October 22, 1803 in Dorchester County, Maryland, died November 13, 1887 in Pickaway County, Ohio, daughter of Thomas Hurst (1778) and Nancy Williams. Children, born Monroe Township, Pickaway County, Ohio:

        (1) Thomas Hays, born June 27, 1827, died March 10, 1902. Married July 9, 1848 to Clarissa W. Girton, born October 9, 1825, died June 3, 1884 in Linn County, Kansas. Five children.

        (2) Wesley Hays, born c.1830

        (3) Sarah A. Hays, born c.1839

        (4) Levi Hays, born c.1841; married May 1, 1862 to Amanda Busich.

    c.   Charles Hays, died February, 1833. Married August 17, 1816 to Margaret Harris.

    d.   Samuel Hays, born July 5, 1790, died March 18, 1857. Married March 8, 1821 to Jemima Rittenhouse.

e. Jesse Hays, born April 9, 1791, died September 17, 1872. Married July 27, 1820 to Elizabeth Hurst, born November 17, 1801 in Dorchester County, Maryland, died December 11, 1841, daughter of Thomas Hurst (1778) and Nancy Williams (1781).

f. Nancy Ann W. Hays, married Samuel Reeves.

g. Mary F. Hays, married January 5, 1822 to Thomas Edmonston.

h. Rachel Hays, married April 9, 1831 to Issac Davis.

i. Eleanor B. Hays, married April 7, 1857 to George Wilcox or George Wilkerson.

5. Solomon Hays, married February 22, 1781 Mary Ann Wise.

6. Samuel Hays.

7. Rachel Hays, married to John Ennis.

8. Rebecca Hays, married to George Howard.

9. Hester Hays, married 1774 to William Tomlinson.

10. Dorcas Hays, married to Nathaniel Harris.

11. Elizabeth Hays, married Zephaniah Gaither or Gautres.

CHILD 4

Jeremiah Hays
died 1783

This son of Thomas Hays (1678) and Mary LeMaistre was born in Charles County, although we have yet to determine the date of birth. He received a patent dated December 10, 1747 in Prince George's County for 100 acres known as *Jeremiah's Park*. In 1748, the area in which it was located became Frederick County, and in 1776, Montgomery County. In 1752, Jeremiah patented the *Resurvey on Jeremiah's Park*, containing 475 acres. Over time, Jeremiah obtained title to other lands in the area, upon which are now located the town of Barnesville, as well as Sellman's Station. He could be the same Jeremiah Hays who was married by license dated October 4, 1773 in Frederick County to Priscilla Sprigg (note that a daughter is named Priscilla). Jeremiah died 1783 in Montgomery County, leaving a will dated September 15, 1783, probated October 18, 1783, originally recorded in liber B at folio 142, rerecorded in liber

VMB 1 at page 123, Register of Wills Office. The will directs that the tracts known as *Jeremiah Park* and *Hopson's Choice* be sold. No wife is named, but he names a number of sons and daughters, listed here in the order in which they appeared in the will, which is not necessarily birth order:

1. Richard Hays, married February 11, 1789 in Frederick County to Charlotte Norris.
2. Thomas Hays, married December 2, 1786 in Frederick County to Ann Wilkey.
3. William Hays.
4. Jeremiah Hays, Jr., died c.1812. Moved to Washington County, Maryland. Married October 4, 1773 in Frederick County to Priscilla Sprigg.
5. Levin Hays, moved to Washington County, Maryland.
6. George Hays, with the note in the will "if he shall return."
7. Sarah Hays, married to Stoakes.
8. Elizabeth Hays, married to Clagett.
9. Margaret Hays, married to Hugh Hoskinson.
10. Mary Hays, married to John Rollins.
11. Priscilla Hays, married c.1774 to her cousin, George Bussey Hays, born about 1752 and died c.1823, son of William Hays, Sr. (1720) and Mary Norris. See children listed under the name of their father in next family group.

CHILD 5

William Hays, Sr.
1720-1791

William was a son of Thomas Hays (1678) and his wife Mary LeMaistre of Charles County, and his wife was perhaps Mary Norris. This is apparently the same William Hays who obtained a warrant for land dated April 23, 1744 in Prince George's County, for 90 acres known as *Dow Harbor*. He is believed to have been born about 1720, and on May 10, 1757 purchased 50 acres of *Cool Spring Manor* from George Bussey, located near Barnesville. He had at least four sons and probably daughters; and died about 1791, probably in the Barnesville area of Montgomery County,

Maryland. He left a will in Montgomery County, dated April 13, 1790, probated February 9, 1791, originally recorded in liber E at folio 1, and rerecorded in liber VMB 1 at page 511, Register of Wills Office. The will does not mention a wife, but names three sons, two daughters and two granddaughters. The children were:

1. George Bussey Hays, born about 1752 and died September 6, 1823 at Barnesville. Under his father's will, he inherited 129 acres of *Resurvey on the Addition to Troublesome,* and 50 acres of *Cool Spring Manor.* He was a slave owner and was married twice: first c.1775 to his cousin, Priscilla Hays, daughter of Jeremiah Hays (died 1783), and second March 16, 1797 to Elizabeth Ridgely. According to the 1790 census, he could have had as many as three sons and five daughters, although early households more often than not contained non-family members. He left a will in Montgomery County dated September 26, 1823, probated December 16, 1823, originally recorded in liber N, folio 460, and rerecorded in liber VMB 3 at page 233, Register of Wills Office. In the will, he names his wife Elizabeth and only one son, William H. Hays. The will also refers to children and grandchildren, but does not provide names. His children appear to have included:

   a. William H. Hays, married September 30, 1824 in Montgomery County to Keturah Harding, which may have been a second marriage.

   b. Priscilla Hays, named as a granddaughter in the will of William Hays, Sr., above. Married under license dated September 10, 1796 in Frederick County to Archibald Owings.

   c. Mary Hays, married about April 4, 1801 in Montgomery County to Robert Dent. They appear to have moved to Belmont County, Ohio before 1811 with other family members.

   d. Martha Hays, named as Patty in her grandfather's will; married about March 20, 1804 in Montgomery County to Asa Dent.

   e. Verlinda Hays, named in the will of her grandfather's second wife Elizabeth.

f.   Zachariah Hays, perhaps, born 1778, died 1856. Married May 5, 1802 in Frederick County to Mary Ann Norris, born 1782, died 1854. Both buried in Belmont County, Ohio, where they moved before 1811.

g.   Sarah Hays, married November 7, 1799 in Montgomery County to Joseph Vermillion.

2.   William Hays, Jr., born c.1754, died January 27, 1825 in Baltimore. For many years, he was a grocer at the old Fish Market in the city. Married about December 6, 1798 in Baltimore to Sarah Ryan (or Ryal), born c.1762, died May 12, 1837. With his brother Notley, he inherited under his father's will 120 acres of the *Resurvey on Jeremiah's Park*, originally called *Friendship*. Of Baltimore in 1798, when he signed an agreement with his brother to sell the land they had inherited from their father. William and Sarah had children, including:

a.   Reverdy Hays, born c.1782, died c.1822. He served in the War of 1812 with his brother William, and was a dry goods merchant and a ship owner in Baltimore. The family Bible states that in 1822 Reverdy sailed from Baltimore for St. Thomas on board the schooner *Fame*, owned by him and his father, and was never heard from again. Married May 16, 1811 to Tabitha Fairbairn of Philadelphia, daughter of John Fairbairn and Mary Houston; and had children:

(1)   William Hays, an infant death.

(2)   James Hays, an infant death.

(3)   Martha Jane Hays, single.

(4)   Reverdy William Hays, single.

(5)   Elizabeth Hays, born c.1816, died c.1889; married November 7, 1833 Robert Burns Griffin, born 1810, died 1879, son of Philip Griffin, Jr. and Rachel Johnson. They lived in Baltimore and for a time in Dorchester, Massachusetts, and had eleven children:

(a)   Henry Clay Griffin, born September 5, 1834; married September 8, 1857 to Sarah Virginia Daw; two daughters.

(b)   Robert Burns Griffin, Jr., born December 2, 1836; married to Maggie Carris, born November 5, 1862, died September 2, 1895; no children.

(c) William Wirt Griffin, born December 31, 1838, died June 10, 1915 in Brooklyn, New York. Married November 5, 1872 to Florence Stoakes; six children.

(d) Charles E. Griffin, born March 25, 1841, died July 22, 1890, single.

(e) Reverdy Hays Griffin, born August 29, 1843, died June 18, 1909. Married December 15, 1881 to Julia O'Laughlin; no children.

(f) Houston Fairbairn Griffin, born December 7, 1845, died April 2, 1905

(g) Bessie Griffin, born May 10, 1848, and died August 19, 1907. Married first September 28, 1868 to J. C. S. Fitzpatrick, who died September 11, 1870. Married second February 6, 1872 to William Harrison Weimer; two sons.

(h) Rachel Tabitha Griffin, born September 19, 1850, died August 15, 1885. Married May 17, 1881 to William C. Martin; two children.

(i) Louise Howard Griffin, born March 20, 1853, died August 7, 1908, single.

(j) George Brice Griffin, born September 27, 1855, died September 29, 1899. Married July 16, 1884 to Emma Florence Seymore. No children.

(k) Francis Dane Griffin, born February 22, 1858, died January 8, 1933. Married October 16, 1884 to Elizabeth McKechnie; three daughters.

(6) Mary Hays, married February 27, 1840 to Captain Edward Gould.

b. Elizabeth Hays, married May 14, 1807 Ezekiel Watts. At least one son:

(1) Reverdy Hays Watts, who lived for a time with his grandmother (after 1820) and was married February 10, 1836 in Baltimore to Margaret Plummer.

c.   William Hays, 3rd, died June 30, 1841; married October 22, 1818 to Jane Moran. After the death of William, she claimed bounty land under his service in the War of 1812 and moved to Illinois with their children.

3.   Leonard Hays, born c.1759, of whom more in Chapter 2.

4.   Notley Hays, born April 2, 1762 in the area that was later known as Barnesville, Montgomery County, died December 12, 1842 in Ohio. With his brother William, Jr., he inherited under his father's will 120 acres of the *Resurvey on Jeremiah's Park*, originally called *Friendship*. In 1791, when he and his brother agreed to sell their inheritance, Notley was in Washington County, Maryland. Married by license dated December 2, 1788 in Frederick County to Sarah Rawlings, died April 1, 1842 in Ohio. They were in Washington County as of c.1798 and moved on to Belmont County, Ohio (admitted as a state in 1803). He left a will, in which he named several children and grandchildren, but apparently not all of them. The Hays family folder file at the library of Montgomery County (Maryland) Historical Society contains prints of several pages of the Notley Hays Family Bible, with numerous entries, providing names, events and dates for many family members, from which much of the following was taken, although there is additional information there also. The children included:

a.   Patience Hays, born July 2, 1784; married 1813 to John Burkett.

b.   Mary Ann Hays, born September 29, 1793; deceased prior to the making of her father's will; married 1819 to John Waterman, and had at least one daughter:
(1)   Martha Waterman, who received a bed and bedding under her grandfather's will.

c.   Sarah Hays, born October 24, 1795; married 1814 to Perry Hulse. At least two daughters:
(1)   Adeline Hulse, who received a bed and bedding from her grandfather's estate.
(2)   Ruth Ann Hulse, who received her grandfather's carpet and desk under his will.

d.   William Hays, born December 1, 1797; at least one son:
(1)   John R. Hays, named in his grandfather's will.

e. Levi Hays, born July 4, 1800.

f. George H. Hays, born July 31, 1802, a twin; married 1832 to Hannah Glessner.

g. Notley Hays, born July 31, 1802, a twin, died young.

h. Nancy Mariah Hays, born November 14, 1804. Married January 31, 1828 in Belmont County, Ohio, to Abraham Crouch, born January 19, 1801, died June 15, 1851, son of Robert and Sarah Crouch. Children included:

   (1) Notley Hays Crouch, born 1828, died 1903. Married c.1855 to Sarah Louisa Wiseman, born July 12, 1828 in New Salem, Ohio, and had children.

   (2) Robert Crouch, born December 28, 1830

   (3) Alfred Crouch, born February 14, 1833, died March 30, 1851

   (4) Sarah E. Crouch, born December 23, 1835

   (5) John W. Crouch, born August 29, 1839

   (6) Mary E. Crouch, born March 1, 1841; married December 26, 1872 to William H. Wilson.

   (7) Abigail F. Crouch, born June 5, 1844

i. Notley Hays, born February 17, 1807, second use of the name.

j. Eliza Hays, born August 14, 1809; married 1833 to James Glessner.

k. Mariah Hays, married 1828 to

l. Brice Hays, married 1822 to Eunice Hubbard.

5. Mary Hays, married to Norris.

6. Eleanor Hays, married to Hempstone.

CHAPTER 2

Leonard Hays
1759-1822

Leonard Hays of Barnesville, Montgomery County, was born c.1759 in what was then Frederick County, Maryland, the son of William Hays, Sr., who died c.1791. Leonard was not named in his father's will, perhaps having received from him during his lifetime, or perhaps because he was quite prosperous in his own right, as witnessed by the lands, lots and houses distributed to his children under his will. In any case, the relationship appears to be determined by a bond filed in Montgomery County Land Records dated March 15, 1796, signed by: George B. Hays, Leonard Hays, Notley Hays, William H. Hays, and William Norris (a brother-in-law) to Jesse Harris, in order to secure title to *Harris Lot*, which was not mentioned in the will of William Hays, Sr.

Leonard was married about August 24, 1782 to Eleanor Simmons in Frederick County, and died on September 14, 1822 at Barnesville, leaving a will, which names his children. He served as private, 2nd Co. Upper Battalion Militia, August 30, 1777, War of the Revolution. Leonard's will was dated September 9, 1822, probated October 1, 1822. Originally recorded in Liber N, folio 283, and rerecorded in liber VMB 3 at page 180, Register of Wills Office, Rockville. Under the will, he left land with the house and lot on which they lived to his widow Eleanor for her lifetime, to then pass to his son William Simmons Hays. Abraham, William and Leonard received the lot and houses on which stood the storehouse, blacksmith shop and barn for a period of three years, and then to be sold. Various other bequests were made to his children, who included:

1. Abraham Simmons Hays, born June 12, 1783, of whom more as Child 1.
2. Sarah Hays, born July 17, 1785, died November, 1854. Married May 22, 1804 to William Candler (one report states John Candler; the family Bible states Daniel Candler). Under her father's will, she inherited 20 acres where Asa Nicholson then resided, and lots in Barnesville. Sarah is listed as head of

household in the 1850 census of the Fourth District, apparently widowed. Living with her is Maria L. White, born c.1832, no relationship stated. However, living next door to Sarah is Leonard W. Candler, who is perhaps a son:

a. Leonard W. Candler, born c.1810. Head of household in the 1850 census of the Fourth District, a merchant, living next door to Sarah Candler, probably his mother. He was married January 30, 1834 to Ann Eliza Fisher, born February 12, 1816, daughter of Thomas Fisher (1782) and Amy Cloud Offutt (1795). In 1850, there were three children at home, but the Candler surname does not appear in any census of Montgomery County after that date:

    (1) Felicia E. Candler, born c.1838
    (2) William M. Candler, born c.1840
    (3) Rosana S. V. Candler, born c.1848

3. Samuel Simmons Hays, born April 1, 1787, of whom more as Child 3.

4. Abigail Hays, born June 5, 1789, of whom more as Child 4.

5. Eleanor Hays, born July 13, 1791, died February 8, 1873; buried at Monocacy Cemetery, Beallsville, with her husband. Both of them were originally buried at Barnesville Methodist Church, and moved to Monocacy October 5, 1917. Married June 8, 1815 in Frederick County to Elisha Howard, born c.1790, died April 27, 1874. Elisha served as a Fifth Sergeant under Captain Hackney during the fall of 1814 in the War of 1812. She was named in her father's will to receive the 20 acres he had purchased from Edward Knott, and the house in which Arthur Leaman then lived. In the 1850 census of the Buckeystown District of Frederick County, Elisha Howard was listed as head of household, with his wife Eleanor; they were childless. Living with them were William S. Hays, born c.1840, and John O. Hays, born c.1842, neither yet identified.

6. Leonard Hays, Jr., born July 30, 1793, died April 25, 1864, of whom more as Child 6.

7. William Simmons Hays, born May 9, 1797, died October 24, 1824. Married February 4, 1823 to Eleanor Harding. May have had as many as three sons, one of whom was perhaps:

a. William Simmons Hays, born November 19, 1842

12

CHILD 1

Abraham Simmons Hays
1783-1861

This son of Leonard Hays (1759) and Eleanor Simmons was born June 12, 1783 near or in Barnesville, in Montgomery County, Maryland, and died March 20, 1861 at Lexington, in Lafayette County, Missouri. Married by license dated January 23, 1816 in Montgomery County to Elizabeth E. Tillard, daughter of Colonel Edward Tillard of Barnesville. Under his father's will, he inherited the land in Barnesville purchased from Lewis and Joseph Knott. A newspaper item of March 18, 1815 announced that Abraham S. Hays had been appointed a Justice of the Peace in Montgomery County. They had children born in Montgomery County before moving c.1849 to Lexington, Lafayette County, Missouri:

1. Edward Leonard Hays, born February 8, 1816, died February 13, 1883. His obituary in *Montgomery County Sentinel* titled him "Justice" E. L. Hays. Head of household in the 1850 census of the Fourth District of Montgomery County, Edward L. was a merchant, with $2,500 in personal property. Edward was married in Montgomery County, March 17, 1840 to Sarah West, born July 15, 1811, died December 25, 1868. They settled in Darnestown and owned a farm near Dufief's Mill. He was a Justice of the Peace in Darnestown during 1882. In 1850 they had seven children at home. Living with them was Catherine Mountz, born c.1810, not otherwise identified. The family was next found in the 1860 census of the Fourth District, where Edward was still a merchant, listed as owning $8,000 in real estate and $7,500 in personal property, quite substantial for the period. There were eight children at home, and Catherine Mountz was still with the household. In the Montgomery County Slave Census of 1867-1868, Sarah is listed as owning six slaves of the Brewer family. Edward was next found in the 1870 census of the Fourth District, listed as a farmer with $4,500 in real estate and $1,000 in personal property. Sarah is there, and two of the children. Edward was found as a widower in the 1880 census of the Sixth District of

Montgomery County, with his daughter Bessie (apparently Elizabeth, the youngest) the only one at home. The *Sentinel* reported that Edward L. Hayes was married November 18, 1880 to Anna T. Waring in Washington (a second marriage). She was born March 28, 1837, died January 11, 1910, daughter of Henry B. and Rachel C. Waring; buried at St. Rose Cemetery at Cloppers. The children were:

a. Maria Tillard Hays, born c.1842. Married to Julian Brewer and lived in New Jersey.

b. Mary Catherine Hays, born c.1843. This child is listed as Kate in the 1860 census. Married July 3, 1866 William J. Sloan (church record says John Sloan). No Sloan surname found in census records.

c. Augusta Selby Hays, born c.1845, died December 6, 1869; buried at Darnestown Presbyterian Church with her parents and other family members.

d. Frances Eleanor Hays, born c.1846, died June 1, 1863; buried at Darnestown Presbyterian

e. Edward Pearre Hays, born July 12, 1847, died April 6, 1920; at home in 1870, and under his occupation, listed simply as "gentleman". In the 1900 census of the Potomac District, Edward was found listed as a hotel bookkeeper in the hotel operated by William Babinger (1863) and his brother George Babinger (1865). Edward was listed as having been married for 21 years, although no wife or family were listed. He is the same individual reported in marriage records as E. P. Hays, married by license dated September 18, 1877 to M. E. Dufief. That is Mary E. Dufief, born c.1854, the daughter of Captain John L. Dufief (1817); (see that family in the 1870 census of the Fourth District).

f. Arthur Hays, born c.1849; not at home in 1860

g. Eugene Hays, born c.1850; not at home in 1860

h. William Clinton Hays, born c.1851

i. Sarah Willson Hays, born c.1853. Married April 27, 1875 in Newark, New Jersey to Henry Atterbury of Brooklyn, New York.

j. Elizabeth Estep Hays, born c.1855; at home in 1870. At home in 1880 with her widowed father, and listed as teaching school; there listed as Bessie, of the proper age.

2. Sarah Eleanor Hays, born February 5, 1819, died June 5, 1849; married Doctor Horace Willson, and moved to Missouri with the family.

3. William Tillard Hays, born February 18, 1821, died January 3, 1887, moved to Missouri with other family members. Married July 18, 1865 to Alice Belle Ward and had four children.

4. Martha Maria Hays, born June 6, 1823, died September, 1840; married November 7, 1839 to John L. Nicholls.

5. Abraham Simmons Hays, Jr., born August 19, 1825, died January 9, 1892. Married January 1, 1873 to Mary E. Davis.

6. Elizabeh Hays, a twin, born January 25, 1828; records of St. Peter's Church, Poolesville.

7. Mary Hays, a twin, born January 25, 1828

8. Alcinda Hays, born December 11, 1830, died March 22, 1852. Records of St. Peter's Church, Poolesville.

9. Richard Estep Hays, born May 14, 1837, died November 13, 1929. Married November 23, 1869 to Lizzie B. Williams, who died July 21, 1910, and had four children.

CHILD 3

Samuel Simmons Hays
1787-1857

This son of Leonard Hays (1759) and Eleanor Simmons was born April 1, 1787 in Maryland, died September 5, 1857. Under his father's will, he received the land on which he then lived, which had been purchased from Alexander Reed and others, as well as land purchased from Thomas Drane, and the house and lot in Barnesville purchased from Samuel Hilton. Head of household in the 1850 census of the Third District of Montgomery County, Samuel was a merchant, with $2,000 in personal property. He was married October 28, 1812 in Montgomery County to Anne Rawlings, born September 7, 1796, died March 8, 1855, daughter of Thomas Rawlings and Elizabeth Fulks (1769). In 1850, they had three children at home, and we have identified additional children from other sources. The Hays Family file in the library of the Montgomery County Historical Society, Rockville, Maryland, contains a family group sheet prepared by Erma M. Brown of Burbank, California. It contains the family of Thomas N. Hays, born March 4, 1820, married August 22, 1843 in Belmont County, Ohio to Ruth Jane Barnes, born there c.1826, and their ten or eleven children. The group sheet reports the parents of Thomas N. Hays as being Samuel S. Hays and Ann Rawlins, which we believe to be incorrect. Attached to the group sheet is additional data indicating that Thomas N. Hays could have been born in Montgomery, Davies County, Indiana, rather than Montgomery County, Maryland. Note that there was a son Thomas L. Hays, born 1816, who lived to adulthood in this family, it being unlikely that a second son would bear the same given name. Note also, earlier, that the Belmont County, Ohio families appeared to be principally descended from Notley Hays (1762) and Sarah Rawlings, roughly a generation earlier than Samuel Simmons Hays of 1787, here discussed. The children were:

1. John H. T. Hays, born October 8, 1813, died June 23, 1857; married May 22, 1837 at St. John's Catholic Church, Forest Glen, Montgomery County, to Eleanor M. Jones, born November 13, 1820, died April 21, 1900; buried at St. Mary's in Barnesville. Church records state that "he will not prevent his wife nor his children from observing the rules of the Catholic Church." This is perhaps the same John Hays found as head of household in the 1850 census of Frederick County, in the Petersville District, John was a merchant, born c.1817. His wife was Ellen (Eleanor ?), born c.1820, and they had five children. He was also a slave-holder, listed with five in 1850. Eleanor was found as head of household in the 1860 census of the Third District of Montgomery County, born c.1821, and apparently widowed, with five children. She was next found in the 1870 census of the Third District, with four of the children still at home. In the 1880 census, she was listed as Mrs. Ellen Hays, married (no indication of being widowed), with the youngest and eldest daughters still at home. Children included:
    a.   Samuel B. Hays, born c.1841

16

b. Laura J. Hays, born c.1843; with her mother in 1860, 1870 and 1880. Married to George W. Bowlen.

c. John T. Hays, born c.1845

d. Florence Elizabeth Hays, born c.1849, died September 27, 1921; buried at Monocacy with her husband. Married in Montgomery County by license dated January 31, 1874 to John Spinks Gott, born January 24, 1848, died August 17, 1923, son of Richard S. Gott, Jr. (1808) and Mary Elizabeth Trundle (1816). They were listed in the 1880 census of the Medley District, with two children. They next appeared in the 1900 census for the Eleventh District, with three sons at home, and the notation that there had been four children born, with three still living. The children were:

(1) Richard Brook Gott, born c.1874, died May 18, 1961; buried Monocacy Cemetery. Married Nellie McDonald, born c.1874, died June 2, 1944; buried with her husband.

(2) John Forest Gott, born c.1879; listed as a school teacher in the 1900 census.

(3) Samuel Roger Gott, born June 23, 1882, died May 28, 1919; buried at Monocacy Cemetery.

(4) M. Luella Gott, died September 21, 1888; buried at Monocacy, and apparently the missing fourth child.

e. Mary Alice Hays, born born August 15, 1850, died December 30, 1925; married to her cousin, Thomas Leonard Hays, Jr., born June 6, 1854, died March 27, 1902, buried at St. Mary's Church in Barnesville, Montgomery County, Maryland. He was listed as head of household in the 1880 census, a farmer, with a wife, Mary, born c.1853. In the 1900 census of the Eleventh District, Town of Barnesville, we found Thomas L. Hays, this same individual, with his wife Mary. He was listed as a salesman, and they had been married 29 years, with two children, apparently twins, both living and at home:

(1) Joseph L. Hays, born June, 1883

(2) Leo Hays, born June, 1883

     f.   Georgiana Hays, probably. This child died of catarrh in the Petersville District, during July, 1850 at age four months.

     g.   Harriet Levanda Hays, born July 5, 1853 (or July 26, 1851; records of St. Peter's Church, Poolesville), died July 25, 1926.

2.   Thomas Leonard Hays, born November 20, 1816, died October 4, 1873, and is buried at Monocacy Cemetery. He is buried with other identified children of this family, and is therefore believed to be a son of Samuel Simmons Hays. Married May 12, 1846 to Mary Tabitha Pearre, born February 19, 1826, died April 9, 1884; buried with her husband. He was first found as head of household in the 1850 census of Frederick County, in the Buckeystown District, with his wife and two children. Thomas was a slave-owner, with three listed. In the 1880 census of the Medley District, we found the household of T. L. Hays, with his wife, his mother, and four sisters living in the household. None of these names were found in earlier census records, although they were all born before 1860. Mary was the mother, a widow, and her children included:

     a.   Anna Catherine Hays, born c.1847; married to Luther M. Bready and had two children.

     b.   May Hays, born August 10, 1849, died September 10, 1918, single; buried at Monocacy with parents.

     c.   Virginia Hays, born c.1851, died April 28, 1930; buried with her parents at Monocacy. Married Albert Anderson.

     d.   Mary Thomas Hays, born February 28, 1853, died May 15, 1912. Married to E. Tobias Bready and had children:

         (1)   John Tilden Bready.

         (2)   Guy Pearre Bready, born c.1882

         (3)   Litty Louise Bready.

         (4)   Mary Elizabeth Naomi Bready.

     e.   Thomas Leonard Hays, Jr., born June 6, 1854, died March 27, 1902, buried at St. Mary's Church in Barnesville, Montgomery County, Maryland. He was listed as head of household in the 1880 census, a farmer, with a wife, Mary, born c.1853. He was married to his cousin, Mary Alice Hays, born August 15, 1850, died December

30, 1925, daughter of John H. T. Hays (1813) and Eleanor M. Jones. In the 1900 census of the Eleventh District, Town of Barnesville, we found Thomas L. Hays, this same individual, with his wife Mary. He was listed as a salesman, and they had been married 29 years, with two children, apparently twins, both living and at home. There is also a reported marriage by license dated November 16, 1918 between Thomas Leonard Hays, Jr. and Kathleen Frances Gott, born April 5, 1896, died December 26, 1981, buried at St. Mary's, Barnesville; daughter of Benjamin Nathan Gott (1856) and Anna Mary Scholl (1859), and had two children. The two children from the first reported marriage, and one from the second were:

(1)   Joseph L. Hays, born June, 1883
(2)   Leo Hays, born June, 1883
(3)   Thomas L. Hays, of Cincinnati, Ohio in 1981

f.   Clara Pearre Hays, born March 7, 1859, died February 13, 1927. Married by license dated November 16, 1880 to George Vernon Davis, born February 3, 1857, died April 19, 1924, son of Isaac Howard Davis (1818) and Catherine Miles (1821). They had children:

(1)   Ira Lynnwood Davis, born September 4, 1881, baptized December 4, 1881 near the Mountain Methodist Church, died May 24, 1960; buried at Hyattstown Methodist Church with his wife. Married to Carrie Olivia Warfield, born December 15, 1887, died June 2, 1940, daughter of Luther Day Warfield (1852) and Ella Belle Tabler (1861). At least a son:

(a)   Lynnwood Davis, born 1916, died 1977. Married to Mary Jane Hartman and had children:
1.   Sherwin Davis, born 1949
2.   Susan Davis, born 1952
3.   Timothy Davis, born 1960

(2)   Mary Catherine Davis, born October 20, 1882, died 1976; married Charles Cunningham Rhodes, Jr.

(3)   Clara Lena Davis, born December 3, 1884, died October 25, 1919. Perhaps the same who was married December 21, 1907 at her family home near

19

Hyattstown to Oscar M. Fogle, a teacher, and had at least four children.

g. Harriet Abigail Hays, born c.1860. Probably the same married January 15, 1883 in Montgomery County to John Wallace Davis of Adamstown, born August 17, 1854, son of Isaac Howard Davis (1818) and Catherine Miles (1821). Children:

(1) Notley Hays Davis, born 1883, died June 1, 1953; buried at Monocacy Cemetery with his wife. She was Mary Loretta Brosius, born March 23, 1886, died April 19, 1968, daughter of Charles Thomas Brosius (1847) and Laura Virginia Trundle (1851). Three children:

(a) Mary Loretta Davis, born November 18, 1911 and married May 29, 1934 to Leonard Jerome Offutt, born June 7, 1910, and had eight children, including:

1. Leonard Jerome Offutt, Jr.: April 26, 1935

(b) Laura Virginia Davis, born December 1, 1914; married January 2, 1939 to Donald L. Riley and had two children.

(c) Notley Hays Davis, Jr., born February 16, 1919

(2) Leona May Davis, born March 20, 1885, died October 9, 1960. Birth records of St. Peter's Church in Poolesville list the parents of Leona May Davis as James Walter Davis and wife, which we can not now explain. Marriage records of St. Peter's report this child as Louise May Davis. Married February 15, 1908 at *Maple Lane* to John Dutrow Linthicum, born 1881, died August 8, 1953; both buried at Monocacy Cemetery, where she is listed as Leona May. They had at least six children.

(3) Louise Pearre Davis, born May 10, 1886, died October 19, 1968. Married April 5, 1910 to John William Brosius, born November 14, 1884, died June 18, 1945; buried at Monocacy, son of Charles Tho-

mas Brosius (1847) and Laura Virginia Trundle (1841). Children:

(a) John William Brosius, Jr., born November 7, 1919. Married first September 6, 1945 Merle A. Fair, born in Sydney, Australia, and had three children. Married second in 1945 Alicia Duarte. Known as Bill, he and his brother Louie (next) were well-known builders and developers in both Frederick and Montgomery Counties, operating as Brosius Brothers, and achieved national attention with the introduction of their largest project, *Lake Linganore*, in Frederick County.

(b) Louie Brosius, born August 27, 1922 at Adamstown, Maryland. Served in the Marines in World War 2; married Angie Feire and had four children (see above also).

    1. Carmen Anna Brosius, born May 28, 1950

    2. Anita Louise Brosius, born May 23, 1952

    3. Myra Brosius, born December 24, 1955

    4. Louie Jarboe Brosius, Jr., born January 20, 1961

(c) Viola Brosius.

(d) Minnie Brosius.

(4) John Wallace Davis, Jr., born October 8, 1886, died July 20, 1971 at Montgomery General Hospital; buried at Monocacy Cemetery with his wife. She was Margaret J. VanSise, born April 12, 1893 in Ohio, died September 11, 1988 at Rockville Nursing Home. Her obituary names two sons from a first marriage; Walter H. Magruder of Rockville, and Thomas F. Magruder of Sacramento; as well as Davis children. The two Magruder children are mentioned in the obituary of John Wallace Davis, Jr. as step-sons. Children included:

(a) Harriet Jane Davis, born 1921, died October 19, 1923, buried with her parents.

(b) John Wallace Davis, III, born July 29, 1924. He was married August 2, 1947 to Frances Vivian Ray, born June 7, 1928, died June 21, 1999 at Shady Grove Hospital, Rockville, Maryland, the daughter of George Franklin Ray, Jr. and Nannie A. King (1905). Four children, with places of residence given in the obituary of their mother:

1. John Wallace Davis, IV, of Virginia, born 1950
2. Charles Thomas Davis, of Ohio, born 1952
3. Amelia D. Davis, born 1955, married to Krebs, of Baltimore.
4. Alan Clark Davis of Finksburg, Maryland, born 1960; married Paulette Campbell.

(c) Margaret VanSise Davis, born July 29, 1924; married to Stuart Campbell Angevine. Birth date is in error, or she is a twin of John Wallace Davis, III.

(d) Leonard Isaac Davis, born August 27, 1928. Married to Dorothy Smith.

(5) Minnie Abigail Davis, born May 23, 1890, died June 5, 1980; buried in the plot of her brother John Wallace Davis, Jr. Married July 11, 1911 to Samuel Brooks Hays. Perhaps a daughter is buried with her:

(a) Virginia Lorraine Hays, born July 31, 1919, died June 6, 1970

(6) Viola Estelle Davis, born June 24, 1894, died 1983. Married December 27, 1919 to Julian Victor Emmert at *Maple Lane*.

(7) Leonard Isaac Davis, born September 17, 1896 and died in 1970. Confirmed at age 16 on November 18, 1913 at Christ Church. Married April 21, 1923 to Eleanor H. Crowther and had a child:

(a) Carol Davis, born 1928 and married to George Bonar.

(8) Thomas Marshall Davis, born April 26, 1905, died November 13, 1997. Married February 25, 1925 Regina Leona Steadman and had children:

    (a) Thomas Marshall Davis, Jr., born September 18, 1925, died November 13, 1996; married Patricia Keller and had four children.

    (b) Mary Regina Davis, born September 28, 1931 at Adamstown in Frederick County. Married August 13, 1950 to Holmes Austin Dutrow, son of Ignatius Dutrow and Mary Thomas, and had six children.

3. Elizabeth Eleanor Hays, born February 22, 1818, died January 30, 1855, of whom more in Chapter 3.

4. Zachariah William Hays, born February 4, 1822

5. Sarah Ann Hays, born December 28, 1823, died January 17, 1847, single.

6. Samuel Simmons Hays, Jr., born April 2, 1826, a teacher, died July 16, 1910, single; buried at Monocacy Cemetery. In the 1850 census of the Third District, living in the household of Richard W. Williams (1815). In the 1860 census for the Third District, he was listed as owning $200 in real estate and $5,100 in personal property, a schoolmaster, surname spelled Hayes, living with John R. Ward (1831). In the Montgomery County Slave Census of 1867-1868, Samuel S. Hays is listed as owning two slaves. In the 1870 census of the Third District, we read the entry as Samuel P. Hays, but of the proper age to be this same individual. He was there listed as a farmer, with $8,050 in real estate and $3,310 in personal property. His sister Harriet A. Hays (following) was living with him, keeping house. Samuel was found living alone, single, a farmer, in the 1880 census of the Medley District. In the 1900 census, Samuel S. was listed as head of household, with his widowed sister Harriet and one of her children living with him. He was there listed single, and as a capitalist. He served for a time as Magistrate of Barnesville.

7. George R. Hays, born c.1827, died November 13, 1888 and buried at Monocacy Cemetery. His obituary in the *Sentinel* states that he was a merchant and farmer near Dickerson Sta-

tion, and that he left a wife and seven children. We place him in this family due to the time frame, Jane Sween's chart in the family file at the Historical Society library, and the Monocacy burials. He was not found in any census records, however. His wife was Sarah A. Thomas, born 1830, died 1894, and buried with her husband. In the same family plot were four other individuals, believed to be children of this couple (the second through fifth listed). The children may have included:

a.   Laura Virginia Hays, perhaps, born c.1859, died January 26, 1930; buried at Monocacy Cemetery at Beallsville with her husband. Baptismal records of Montgomery Methodist Circuit state that she was baptized December 16, 1862, daughter of George W. and Mrs. Hays. Witnesses were parents and Fannie Hempstone. Records of St. Peter's Church at Poolesville report that she was a daughter of George Hays and Mrs. Hays, and was married October 23, 1879 to Charles Edgar Poole, born September 26, 1854, died December 23, 1937, son of James Franklin Poole (1831) and Ann Eliza Hoskinson (1837). Charles and Laura were listed soon after their marriage living alone in the 1880 census of the Cracklin District, but were not found in the 1900 census. Children:

   (1)   Elsie May Poole, born August 10, 1880, died September 21, 1881; buried Monocacy with her father.
   (2)   Charles Vernon Poole, born 1881, died 1939
   (3)   Edgar Lynwood Poole, born 1883, died 1919
   (4)   Anna Lee Poole, born 1888, died 1961
   (5)   Hays Rawlings Poole, born 1890, died 1940

b.   Otho Thomas Hays, born 1861, died 1884.

c.   Sarah Ida Hays, born 1863, died April 26, 1927 at Hagerstown, Maryland.

d.   Mary Emma Hays, born January 15, 1868, died February 3, 1913. Married to Joseph St. Clair Wiggins.

e.   Samuel Edward Hays, born 1873, died September 6, 1932.

f.   Hattie A. Hays, married at the home of her father October 30, 1877 to John C. Lamar, born September 13, 1856 on his father's farm near Adamstown, Frederick County, son of Benoni Lamar and Mary C. Thomas. John operated Lamar & Son, General Merchandise, at Licksville. Not found in any census record, but had one son:

(1) Clarence H. Lamar.

8. Harriet Abigail Hays, born April 5, 1830, died May 23, 1906; buried at Monocacy with other family members. Living with her brother Samuel as late as 1870 (above). Married September 14, 1874 to Edward Baker. Harriet was widowed before 1900 (census of Eleventh District), when she was found in the household of her brother Samuel S. Hays, above. She was there noted as having had no children. Living in the same household was Mary E. Baker, born March, 1870, not otherwide identified.

9. William Notley Hays, born March 18, 1834, died February 9, 1909; buried at Monocacy Cemetery. In the 1860 census of the Third District, surname spelled Hayes, listed as a clerk, living in the household of Benjamin S. White (1828), a merchant. In the Montgomery County Slave Census of 1867-1868, William is listed as owning one slave. In the 1870 census of the Third District, William was listed as a village merchant, with $6,000 in personal property, living in the hotel operated by James Uriah Miles (1821) at Poolesville. William was next found as head of household in the 1880 census of the Medley District, a merchant, single. Living with him was James V. Norris, a clerk, born c.1836. William N. Hays was then found in the 1900 census of the Third District, town of Poolesville, listed as a capitalist, single, boarding in the household of Julius Hall (1872), the local mail carrier.

10. Franklin T. Hays, perhaps, born c.1839

CHILD 4

Abigail Hays
1857-

This daughter of Leonard Hays (1759) and Eleanor Simmons was born died May 10, 1857. Married June 14, 1809 in Frederick County, Maryland to William Trail, son of William Trail (d/1783) and Frances Northcroft. He owned a tavern at Barnesville, Montgomery County, Maryland, and died c.1833, having been first married to Priscilla Shaw. Abigail inherited 120 acres of land and lots in Barnesville from her father under his will. She was listed as head of household in the 1850 census of the Third District, of an age to be this individual. Living with her are several individuals whom we believe to be part of her family, including a daughter, who is apparently widowed. Also living with Abigail was Sarah Trail, born c.1805, not identified. Division of the lands of William Trail, deceased, liber BS4, folio 283, Montgomery County, lists nine of his children. At least three children from his first marriage, and several from the marriage to Abigail Hays:

1.   Reverdy Hays Trail, born February 11, 1821 (or 1827), baptized February 10, 1828. Married November 23, 1865 in Baltimore County, Maryland to Emily Morrison. Reverdy Hays Trail was named for his maternal great uncle Reverdy Hays, who, according to a family Bible record, left Baltimore in 1822 as supercargo on the schooner *Fame*, owned by his father William Hays, bound for St. Thomas and was never heard from again. At least a daughter:
     a.   Mary Ernesta Trail, born April 28, 1858

2.   Mary Jane Trail, born c.1823, married December 15, 1841 to Joseph Hawkins. She appeared in the 1850 census for the Medley District, in a household headed by her mother Abigail. Also living in the household was Sarah Trail, born c.1805, which may be Sarah Perry Trail, an older daughter of Abigail, although the birth year is not consistent. At the time, Mary J. (Trail) Hawkins appeared to have four daughters. Mary J. appeared next as head of household in the 1860 census for the Medley District, with her sister Sarah (Sally) still living with her, and the three youngest children still at home. Children:
     a.   Laura V. Hawkins, born c.1843. Married February 2, 1859 to Richard T. Pyles, born c.1832. He was head of household in the 1860 census of the Third District, a merchant, with Laura and their first child. The surname was there spelled Piles, which is perhaps incorrect. In the 1870 census for the Third District, Richard T. Pyles was listed without a wife, perhaps widowed. Living with him

were two children, as well as his mother-in-law Mary J. Hawkins, his sister-in-law Frances E. Hawkins, and Laura's aunt, Sarah Perry Trail. After the death of Laura, Richard T. Pyles was married secondly to her sister Frances E. Hawkins (1847) and had children, which see below. The children of Laura were:

(1) Clagett Pyles, born c.1860; married April, 1892 in Baltimore to Mary V. Middlekauff of that city.

(2) Annie E. Pyles, born c.1861; probably the same who was married July 23, 1884 to Edward E. Crockett. They appeared in the 1900 census for the Bethesda District, where she was listed as born September, 1867 (different, but not unusual for census), and he was listed as born July, 1860, and a school teacher. They had been married sixteen years, having had five children, only two of whom survived and were still at home:

(a) Bessie Crockett, born August, 1887

(b) Annie L. Crockett, born October, 1890

b.   Elizabeth M. Hawkins, born c.1845

c.   Frances E. Hawkins, born c.1847; apparently married as his second wife to Richard T. Pyles, who was first married to her sister Laura V. Hawkins (above). Richard and Frances appeared in the 1880 census of the Medley District, where he was listed as a store-keeper. Living with them was Annie Pyles, born to his first marriage (see above), and three children born to the marriage to Frances. Also living there was Mary Hawkins, born c.1822, listed as a stepmother (actually mother-in-law, the mother of Frances E. Hawkins). The *Montgomery County Sentinel* of May 17, 1889 reported that Richard T. Pyles, age 58, died at his home in Barnesville on May 12, 1889, a merchant of that town, married twice, and left a widow and several children. In the 1900 census, Frances E. appears as head of household in the Eleventh District, widowed, with three children at home, as well as her mother Mary J. Hawkins. Frances is listed as a dry goods merchant. Children born to Frances were:

(1) Percy L. Pyles, born c.1872; a dry goods merchant, like his mother

(2) Joseph Pyles, born c.1874; not at home in 1900

(3) Lottie V. Pyles, born c.1879

(4) Richard G. Pyles, born c.1884

d. Mary C. Hawkins, born c.1849

CHILD 6

Leonard Hays, Jr.
1793-1864

This son of Leonard Hays (1759) and Eleanor Simmons was born July 30, 1793 in Maryland, died April 24, 1864. Head of household in the 1850 census of the Third District of Montgomery County, Leonard was listed as a merchant, with $14,200 in personal property, a wife Eliza, born c.1807, and eight children. Leonard Hays was married May 26, 1825 to Eliza Sprigg Poole, born June 28, 1807, died July 21, 1874, daughter of John Poole (1768) and Priscilla W. Sprigg. He and Eliza were first buried at Barnesville Methodist Church cemetery, and moved on October 5, 1917 to Monocacy Cemetery at Beallsville. Leonard and Eliza were next found in the 1860 census, although there the surname was recorded as Hayes. Leonard was listed as a farmer, with $30,000 in real estate and $39,000 in personal property, quite well-to-do for the time period. There were five children at home. In the Montgomery County Slave Census of 1867-1868, Eliza Hays is listed as owner of twenty-seven slaves, all listed by name and age, ranging from 1 year old to 64 years old. That record can be found at the library of the Montgomery County Historical Society in Rockville. In the 1870 census of the Third District, Eliza is a widow, listed with $3,000 in real estate and $1,000 in personal property. Five of the children are still living at home, and each is listed with property, apparently having inherited from their father. The children included, at least:

1. Priscilla Eleanor Elizabeth Hays, born June 27, 1827, died September 30, 1828.

2. Sarah Paulina Hays, born February 21, 1829, died October 7, 1892. Married December 8, 1857 to Nathan T. Talbott, born c.1819, son of Henry W. Talbott and Sarah Benson. We found the couple first in the 1880 census of the Medley District, village of Barnesville, where he was listed as a hotel keeper. No children were listed. In the 1900 census for the Eleventh District, village of Barnesville, Nathan T. was listed as a widower, and a landlord.

3. Eleanor Leonard Hays, born November 19, 1831, died October 19, 1891. Married January 26, 1854 to William Thomas Poole, born October 11, 1829, son of John Poole and Sarah Dickerson (1802). They were found in the 1860 census for the First District, where he was listed as an Agent, with $2,000 in personal property. She was there listed at 25 years old, somewhat different than the birth year reported in the 1850 census, but not unusual. There were then two children. We did not find the family in any later census. The children were:

    a. Algernon Poole, born c.1857, died 1906; buried at Monocacy Cemetery. Married May 17, 1886 to Mary Waters, born c.1864, died December 18, 1951; buried with her husband. They were found in the 1900 census for the Eleventh District, married for fourteen years, having had five children, all still living, with four at home. There appear to have been others, buried at Monocacy with their parents; note that Edward was a stillbirth, and Mildred lived only two years, and both were perhaps not included in the number of children born. Children:

        (1) William T. Poole, born April 4, 1887, died November 15, 1893
        (2) Mary W. Poole, born c.1890
        (3) Edward Poole, stillbirth May 21, 1893
        (4) Mable Poole, born c.1895
        (5) Wilson Poole, born c.1896
        (6) Sarah Dickerson Poole, born November 23, 1899, died May 19, 1985.
        (7) Mildred Poole, born December 23, 1902, died 1904

    b. Hays Poole, born c.1859

c. Sallie D. Poole, married June 2, 1885 William F. Bevan; not found in any census record.

d. Leonard Hempstone Poole, married Mrs. Sophia Jackson.

4. Priscilla John Hays, born February 9, 1835, died July 27, 1909; buried at Monocacy Cemetery; at home in 1870, with $1,000 in real estate. In the 1880 census of the Medley District, in the village of Barnesville, we found Mrs. P. Poole listed with L. I. Hays. He was head of household, single; she was a widow, listed as his sister. He was Leonard I. Hays, listed following. Priscilla was married October 1, 1860 to Reginald Poole, although she was listed with her maiden name at home in the 1870 census. Monocacy Cemetery records report that Reginald Poole was buried there April 11, 1861, having died at the age of 28 years, 1 month and 7 days. He was the son of Dr. Thomas H. Poole.

5. Elizabeth Medora Hays, born December 11, 1836 and died January 18, 1859. *Sentinel* obituary lists her as Miss Eliza Medora Hays (single). First buried at Barnesville Methodist Church cemetery, and moved October 5, 1917 to Monocacy Cemetery. *Monocacy Cemetery, Beallsville, Montgomery County, Maryland*, by Elizabeth R. Frain lists this individual as Eliza Medora Hays Howard, with the note that Howard is not on the stone. We believe she was unmarried.

6. Leonard Isaac Jones Hays, born September 8, 1838, died August 20, 1901; buried at Monocacy Cemetery, Beallsville. At home in 1870, with $2,000 in real estate. Married October 24, 1888 to Mary Eliza Waters White, born October 2, 1867, died January 15, 1960, buried with her husband, daughter of Richard Thomas White (1829) and Mary Elizabeth Waters (1830). They were found in the 1900 census of the Eleventh District, town of Barnesville, having been married for twelve years, and had by then had three children, all living, and at home. Children included:

a. Leonard Hays, born August 28, 1889, and died May 10, 1982, a doctor; buried at Monocacy in the family plot. He interned in London and was a surgeon in the British Navy early in the first World War, later serving in the same capacity in the United States Navy. He was single.

30

b. Richard Shirley Hays, born September 27, 1891, and died August 3, 1973; buried at Monocacy Cemetery with his parents. He was elected to the State Legislature in 1932, serving a two-year term; was chairman of the Montgomery County Board of Education; and president of the Board of Commissioners of the town of Barnesville. His obituary stated that he spent his entire life on the farm settled by his ancestors in 1747. He and his two brothers owned a dairy farm in the Barnesville area for more than sixty years. He was single.

c. Frederick Sprigg Hays, born July 23, 1893, died October 17, 1973 at Frederick Memorial Hospital. Records of St. Peter's Church, Poolesville; buried at Monocacy in the family plot. Married October 10, 1923 to Eleanor Merryman Ray, born November 24, 1899 at Sweetwater, Texas, died August 26, 1994; buried with her husband; daughter of Benton and Elizabeth Ray. The obituary of Eleanor names her children, and seven grandchildren, with their place of residence as of 1994: Eleanor T. Lawrence of Florida; Frederick H. Tolbert of Germantown; Richard L. Tolbert; Ineke L. Schneider; Martha L. Ward; and Shirley L. Prasada-Roa, all of Barnesville; and John C. Tolbert of Puerto Rico. They had three children:

   (1) Frederick Sprigg Hays, Jr., born September 27, 1928. Served as a Lieutenant in Korea; killed in action August 22, 1952 (not buried at Monocacy).

   (2) Elizabeth Ray Hays, married to Tolbert.

   (3) Mary White Hays, married to Lok.

7. Richard Poole Hays, born December 18, 1840, died April 8, 1912; buried at Monocacy Cemetery. His name appears on a large stone at the cemetery, commemorating the Maryland soldiers who served in the Confederate Army. He served as a private in Company B, 35th Virginia Cavalry. At home in 1870, listed as a country merchant, with $2,500 in real estate. Apparently the same listed in the 1880 census of the Medley District simply as Richard, although the age is five years different. Keeping store, with a wife Bettie, born c.1855 and two children. Married February 4, 1875 to Bettie G. Batson, born

March 25, 1855, died February 23, 1923; buried with her husband, youngest daughter of Leonard N. Batson of Howard County. Notes of Jane Sween in the Historical Society library, and the Hays family Bible, report her name as Elizabeth Baldwin. Head of household in the 1900 census of the Eleventh District of Montgomery County, he was listed as a salesman, with his wife and seven children. There were others:

a. Millie Hays, born c.1876; not at home in 1900. We believe it is possible that the proper name of this child was Eleanor Medora Hays, with the middle name having been taken from that of her father's sister, Elizabeth Medora Hays, a name which does not occur elsewhere in the family. If so, she was married to Hugh Peter Hill, Sr., born 1873, died February 13, 1964. Eleanor Medora was born c.1875, died May 29, 1959 and both are buried at Monocacy in the same plot with Frederick Albert Hays who, if we are correct, was her brother.

b. Richard Poole Hays, infant death; born c.1877, buried December 2, 1878 at Monocacy.

c. Infant death, buried February 15, 1879 at Monocacy.

d. Nana P. Hays, born January 16, 1880; died July 19, 1926 at the state sanitorium; buried at Monocacy Cemetery.

e. Elizabeth Z. Hays, born February 13, 1882; died September 1, 1926, single. Buried at Monocacy Cemetery.

f. Leonard Batson Hays, born March 26, 1884; died December 27, 1947. Buried at Monocacy Cemetery.

g. Richard Kenton Hays, born January 5, 1886, died July 5, 1952; buried at Monocacy Cemetery.

h. Frederick Albert Hays, born c.1889, died October 21, 1959; buried at Monocacy with his wife. She was Alice R. Cole, born November 24, 1919, died September 29, 1990.

i. Sarah P. Hays, born c.1892

j. Hink L. Hays, born c.1895, according to the 1900 census. This is perhaps Robert Lee Hays, born September 8, 1895, died June 25, 1920, and buried at Monocacy with his parents.

8. William Thomas Hays, born March 11, 1843, died young.

9. Samuel Brook Hays, perhaps, killed August 26, 1862 at Waterford, Virginia, Civil War. Private, Co. A, 35th Virginia Cavalry, CSA.

10. Frederick Poole Hays, born March 18, 1846, died March 20, 1921, buried at Monocacy Cemetery, Beallsville. He was listed as a farmer, single, in the 1870 census of the Third District, owning $6,780 in real estate and $1,263 in personal property. In the same census, Frederick P. Hays was found living at home with his widowed mother, listed as a country merchant. It appears that the census taker counted him in both places. Listed as single, head of household, a farmer, in the 1880 census for the Medley District (Third), with five farm workers. Married February 22, 1881 at the Episcopal Church in Leesburg, Virginia to Ida Lee Hempstone, born October 21, 1854, died May 2, 1946, buried with her husband. She was the daughter of Christian Townley Hempstone, II (1810), and Mary Rebecca Dade (1815). Cemetery records list the name of this individual as Frederick Poole Hays; other sources indicate that his actual name was Frederick Procorus Hays. Records of St. Peter's Church, Poolesville report confirmation of Frederick Procorus Hays on February 16, 1879. The Hays Family file at the Montgomery County Historical Society library in Rockville contains a transcription of entries in the family Bible owned by Frederick P. Hays, copied 1913, which provided valuable information relative to the family. The family appeared in the 1900 census of the Eleventh District of Montgomery County, with six children at home, and all in school The census stated that they had been married for nineteen years, having had only the six children then listed. The children, most of whom are buried at Monocacy Cemetery, were:

    a. Mary Dade Hays, born August 12, 1882, died May 27, 1956. Married June 6, 1906 as his second wife to Reginald James Darby, born 1882, died May 28, 1941, son of James Washington Darby (1851) and Mary Jeanette Dade (1853).

    b. William Reginald Hays, born January 10, 1884, died May 27, 1913, single.

c. Frederick Leonard Hays, born October 30, 1885, died July 26, 1942, single. Records of St. Peter's Church at Poolesville.

d. Robert Townley Hays, born July 17, 1887, died August 18, 1939, single.

e. Lawrence Dade Hays, born September 30, 1890, died September 30, 1966 at Bonita Springs, Florida of cancer, a retired mortgage broker, single.

f. Frederick Poole Hays, Jr., born October 31, 1892, died April 28, 1983. Records of St. Peter's Church, Poolesville. Married October 24, 1923 to Katherine Elizabeth White, born October 23, 1896, died October 29, 1985 in Clearwater, Florida, daughter of Harvey Jones White (1869) and his first wife Ida Dyson (1872); buried at Monocacy Cemetery in Beallsville, Montgomery County, Maryland. No children.

11. Mary Martha Poole Hays, born February 19, 1849, died November 10, 1929; at home as late as 1870. Married January 23, 1873 to John Jones, born c.1839 and lived on the farm known as *Blenheim*, west of Poolesville. John and Mary were found in the 1880 census of the Medley District, with three children. They were next found in the 1900 census of the Third District, with seven children at home, including the earlier three. They were said to have been married for 27 years, having had nine children, seven of them then living, and all at home. The known seven were:

a. Mary C. Jones, born c.1876

b. Leonard Hays Jones, born c.1877

c. Eliza M. Jones, born c.1879

d. Pinkney Jones, born c.1882

e. Elizabeth Jones, born c.1886

f. Eleanor Jones, born c.1888

g. Reginald Jones, born c.1895

12. Alcinda Folins Hays, born December 13, 1851, died November 27, 1852.

CHAPTER 3

Elizabeth Eleanor Hays
1818-1855

This daughter of Samuel Simmons Hays (1787) and Anne Rawlings (1796) was born February 22, 1818 in Montgomery County, and died January 30, 1855. Married February 26, 1835, as his first wife, to John Alexander Trundle, born December 18, 1813 in Montgomery County, and died April 24, 1871; buried at Mt. Olivet in Frederick; son of Hezekiah William Trundle (1792) and Christiana Whitaker (1795). He was reportedly a member of the Carrollton Manor Mounted Guards, Confederate forces, Civil War, but was not found listed in *Marylanders in the Confederacy,* by Daniel D. Hartzler. He was married second August 17, 1857 to Martha E. Plummer, born August 8, 1827, died March 1, 1906, the daughter of William Plummer and Elizabeth Howard. Some reports state that he was married second May 6, 1856 to Sarah Ann Lee, and third November 3, 1870 to Mildred Catherine Lee (perhaps sisters), but we can not verify that. He was found as head of household in the 1850 census for the Buckeystown District of Frederick County, with his first wife, Elizabeth, and eight children. They were reportedly born in Montgomery County, although it appears it was more likely Frederick:

1. Hester Ellen Trundle, born August 23, 1836, died January 19, 1925, of whom more as Child 1.
2. Samuel Hezekiah Trundle, born August 29, 1838 of whom more as Child 2.
3. Elizabeth Rawlings Trundle, born April 10, 1840 and died January 5, 1909, of whom more as Child 3.
4. Christianna Whitaker Trundle, born February 2, 1842, died August 31, 1932, of whom more as Child 4.
5. Anna Hays Trundle, born March 12, 1844, of whom more as Child 5.
6. George Thomas Trundle, born December 2, 1846, of whom more as Child 6.

7. Harriet Abigail Trundle, born July 21, 1848, of whom more as Child 7.
8. John L. Trundle, born c.1849 according to the 1850 census, but of whom nothing more is known.
9. Laura Virginia Trundle, born April 5, 1851, of whom more as Child 9.
10. Sarah John Trundle, born December 2, 1853, of whom more as Child 10.

CHILD 1

Hester Ellen Trundle
1836-1925

This daughter of John Alexander Trundle (1813) and Elizabeth Eleanor Hays (1818) was born August 23, 1836, died January 19, 1925. Married November 6, 1856 Algernon Loving Whitaker, born July 1, 1829, died November 4, 1906. Not found in census records of Montgomery County. Reportedly they had six children:
1. Harriet Elizabeth Whitaker, born September 17, 1857, died September 5, 1929, single.
2. Anna Lee Whitaker, born November 5, 1860, died August 10, 1865.
3. Cora John Whitaker, born April 26, 1863, died January 29, 1927. Married October 31, 1900 to Richard Edwin Darby, born February 10, 1862, died September 19, 1938, the son of John William Darby and Ellen Ruth Edelen. Two children, one of whom died at birth; the other young, who was:
   a. Ruth Ellen Darby, born December 27, 1902, died May 14, 1919.
4. Virginia Mildred Whitaker, born July 9, 1866, died May 31, 1929. Married January 22, 1895 Samuel H. Carter, born December 31, 1868, died December 27, 1926, and had children:
   a. Hester L. Carter, born November 27, 1895. Married July 28, 1920 to Robert S. Huey, born October 7, 1893. They had children:
      (1) Robert Carter Huey, born November 27, 1922
      (2) Harvey Lee Huey, born June 9, 1924

       (3) Virginia Mary Huey, born May 11, 1926

       (4) Barbara Ann Huey, born August 5, 1927

b. Beulah Fay Carter, born April 13, 1897, married to A. L. Robinson.

c. Mary Frances Carter, born December 30, 1898. Married April 12, 1922 to Fred Hazelwood, born April 4, 1899. Children:

       (1) Fay Carter Hazelwood; December 30, 1898

       (2) Fred Hazelwood, 3rd; July 26, 1925

5. Beulah Whitaker, born September 25, 1868, single

6. Theresa Whitaker, born May 2, 1871, single

CHILD 2

Samuel Hezekiah Trundle
1838-1882

This son of John Alexander Trundle (1813) and Elizabeth Eleanor Hays (1818) was born August 29, 1838 at Buckeystown, Frederick County, Maryland, died April 11, 1882; buried at Mt. Olivet cemetery, Frederick City. Married October 23, 1866 to Alice Chiswell, born September 29, 1842 in Montgomery County, Maryland, died March 2, 1933; buried at Mt. Olivet; daughter of Joseph Newton Chiswell (1812) and Eleanor White (1822). They had children:

1. Arthur White Trundle, born March 29, 1868, died September 8, 1924. Married January 27, 1903 to Jennie G. Wendel, born October 9, 1869. A child:

a. Margaret Wendel Trundle.

2. Benjamin Chiswell Trundle; probably the same individual who was born March 11, 1870, died August 6, 1889, and is buried at Mt. Olivet.

3. Elizabeth Eleanor Trundle, married to Emory H. Kramer and had two children. Married second March 25, 1909 to J. Edward Myers. Her children were:

a. Myrtle Marie Kramer, married to George K. Ruby.

b. Ollie Leone Kramer, married Howard B. Yost and had children:

(1) Alice Chiswell Yost.
(2) Roger Less Yost.
(3) Thomas Beidleman Yost.
4. Alice Chiswell Trundle, married April 8, 1909 to Forrest Sidney Thackary; two children, one of whom was:
   a. Christine Cora Thackary. Married June 15, 1935 to Sterling D. Balderson.
5. Samuel Hezekiah Trundle, Jr., an infant death.

CHILD 3

Elizabeth Rawlings Trundle
1840-1909

This daughter of John Alexander Trundle (1813) and Elizabeth Eleanor Hays (1818) was born April 10, 1840 and died January 5, 1909 Married January 29, 1861 William Balster Kramer, born January 31, 1836, died November 9, 1921. They had children:
1. John Frederick Kramer, died August 20, 1933. Married to Ella Hartman and second to Nora Miller Coulter.
2. Samuel Brook Hayes Kramer, died October 4, 1933
3. Eleanor Kramer, born October 5, 1867. Married May 5, 1892 to Frank C. Deming, who died July, 1919. They had children:
   a. Florence Deming, born January 3, 1895. Married to Joseph G. Ibach, Jr. and had children:
      (1) Eleanor Lorrain Ibach, born May 23, 1918
      (2) Elizabeth Deming Ibach, born August 18, 1920
   b. Eleanor Jeanette Deming, born March 3, 1897 and married October 27, 1920 to Ralph H. Dean. At least one child:
      (1) Jean Dean, born February 19, 1923
4. William Balster Kramer, 2nd, born January 25, 1870 and died January 27, 1927. Married August 31, 1892 to Martha Ellen Heaton, born December 1, 1868, and died March 25, 1927. Children:
   a. Martha M. Kramer.

b. William Balster Kramer, 3rd, born December 26, 1896. Married June 24, 1925 to Anita J. Humphrey, born November 30, 1896, died January 5, 1933. Children:
   (1) Lawrence Humphrey Kramer, born August 30, 1926
   (2) Joanne Ellen Kramer, born June 17, 1929
   (3) Martin Alvord Kramer, born December 11, 1932
c. James Thomas Kramer, born February 26, 1902. Married June 12, 1929 to Mary Ruth McAdams, born April 2, 1904. Children:
   (1) John McAdams Kramer, born December 23, 1930
   (2) James Thomas Kramer, Jr., born March 15, 1933
   (3) William Balster Kramer, 4th, born December 23, 1935

5. Ledru Rawlings Kramer, born October 16, 1872. Married March 5, 1896 to Florella Deming, and had a child:
a. Blanch Deming Kramer, born January 1, 1897 and married January 2, 1917 to Tim V. Ransom. Two children:
   (1) Rawlings V. Ransom.
   (2) William Kramer Ransom.

6. Bertha Louella Kramer, born February 11, 1879. Married November 12, 1902 to Harry James Haselton, born June 19, 1878, and had at least one daughter:
a. Winifred Mae Haselton, born March 3, 1905 and married June 21, 1929 to James D. Wheatley, born August 3, 1904. Children:
   (1) Eleanor Catherine Wheatley: April 27, 1930
   (2) Jack Haselton Wheatley: July 24, 1934

CHILD 4

Christianna Whitaker Trundle
1842-1932

This daughter of John Alexander Trundle (1813) and Elizabeth Eleanor Hays (1818) was born February 2, 1842, died August 31, 1932. Married January 12, 1869 to Arthur Cromwell, born February 28, 1837, died September 3, 1905. They had children:

1. Carlton Cromwell, born January 3, 1870, died October 27, 1930. Married c.1897 to Clara Tavenner; children:
   a. C. Mehrl Cromwell, born April 27, 1901
   b. Anna Belle Cromwell, born September 5, 1910
2. Cleveland Cromwell, born March 4, 1873; married February 8, 1899 to Mary Elizabeth Fitzsimmons and had four children:
   a. Nannie W. Cromwell, born December 11, 1899 and married March 17, 1923 William Clements Gloyd, born June 20, 1896, son of Samuel Arthur Gloyd (1865) and Sarah Augusta Clements (1863). They had children:
      (1) William Cromwell Gloyd: March 15, 1924
      (2) John Carroll Gloyd, born July 29, 1925, married October 11, 1947 to Ruth Gubbe.
      (3) Sarah Elizabeth Gloyd, born March 19, 1927
      (4) Mary Ann Gloyd, born January 27, 1929
      (5) James A. Hays Gloyd, born January 22, 1931
      (6) Joseph Cleveland Gloyd: December 8, 1932
      (7) Clara Rebecca Gloyd, born August 23, 1936
      (8) Samuel Arthur Gloyd, born March 6, 1938
      (9) Albert Leo Gloyd, born November 16, 1941
   b. E. Joanette Cromwell, born May 14, 1902. Married c.1932 to Elmer Justh and had children:
      (1) Mary Catherine Justh: April 15, 1933
      (2) Joseph Elmer Justh.
      (3) Robert Stanley Justh.
      (4) Helen Martin Justh.
   c. Pearl Cromwell, born July 31, 1903
   d. A. Hays Cromwell, born January 17, 1905
3. Edna Clem Cromwell, born November 3, 1875 and died November 15, 1946 at Frederick, single.
4. A. Hays Cromwell, born November 3, 1877.
5. Richard Cromwell, born April 20, 1880 and died February 11, 1968; buried at Monocacy cemetery. Married November 26, 1902 to Ollie Grace Hoyle born August 13, 1879, died February 9, 1962, the daughter of Joseph Henry Hoyle and Charlotte Ann Jones. At least one daughter and a son:
   a. J. Arthur Cromwell, born August 11, 1903, married June 24, 1931 to Caroline Smith.

b. G. Elizabeth Cromwell, born May 3, 1905. Married April 7, 1926 to Howard Stepp. One child:
    (1) Louisjean Stepp, born January 16, 1934

CHILD 5

Anna Hays Trundle
1844-1925

This daughter of John Alexander Trundle (1813) and Elizabeth Eleanor Hays (1818) was born March 12, 1844, died April 21, 1925; buried at Monocacy cemetery near Beallsville. Married April 24, 1866 to Levin Thomas, born April 9, 1841 in Frederick County, died December 17, 1899 at Gaithersburg, in Montgomery County, buried at family plot in Point of Rocks; son of Otho Thomas and Harriet Elizabeth Rawlings. Levin served as a private in Co. B, 35th Virginia Cavalry, Rosser's Brigade, Confederate Cavalry; captured at Leesburg June 26, 1864; prisoner at Elmira, New York. Received the *Southern Honor Cross* for his service. They had children:

1. John Gertrude Thomas, born February 15, 1867, died January 3, 1935. Married June 28, 1892 to Arthur Thomas Lewis, born February 22, 1864, died January 10, 1942, and buried at Forest Oak cemetery in Gaithersburg, Montgomery County, Maryland. Children:
    a. Clyde Purnell Lewis, born December 5, 1893, died October 11, 1910; buried with his parents.
    b. Gertrude Estelle Lewis, born July, 1897 and baptized January 29, 1899 at Ascension Chapel.
    c. Mabelle Arthur Lewis, born April 30, 1900, married to Hollis W. Andrews and had children:
        (1) Mary Louise Andrews, born December 12, 1918, died January 23, 1919
        (2) Helen Louise Andrews, born August 20, 1922
        (3) Robert Clyde Andrews, born July 23, 1929
2. Emma Reese Thomas, born January 24, 1868 and died January 9, 1930 in Maryland. Married January 10, 1906 Richard Thomas Butler, his second wife. He died January 11, 1952,

the son of Charles Martin Butler and Frances Thomas Spates. Children:

    a.   Kathleen Mabelle Butler, born August 20, 1907 and died January 31, 1928

    b.   Richard Thomas Butler, born February 3, 1910 and married 1933 to Elspeth Jackson. A son:

        (1)   Richard Thomas Butler, 3rd: May 30, 1934

3.   Elizabeth Thomas, born 1870, infant death

4.   John Gordon Thomas, born May 15, 1873, died November 28, 1918. Married January 3, 1895 Ada Thompson. They had children:

    a.   Reese Gordon Thomas, born May 7, 1897. Married July 20, 1916 to Otis G. Clark and had children:

        (1)   William Gordon Clark, born March 7, 1918

        (2)   Carroll Thomas Clark, born February 26, 1923

    b.   Carroll Gordon Clark, born December 29, 1899, died January 5, 1917

    c.   Hester Elizabeth Clark, born November 25, 1902. Married August 23, 1934 to Harold C. Geest. A son:

        (1)   Christopher Clark Geest.

5.   Charles Purnell Thomas, born July 27, 1875, died November 4, 1965 Montgomery County; married 1908 to Clara Reddick.

6.   Harriet Abigail Trundle Thomas, born April 28, 1878. Married Montgomery County, November 1, 1904 to George Lucas Babington, born c.1880 and had children:

    a.   Cornelia Anna Babington, born November 3, 1906, was not married.

    b.   Harriett Estelle Babington, born November 26, 1907. Married F. Harold Harmon, born August 30, 1905, and had children:

        (1)   Norma Estelle Harmon, born March 23, 1928

        (2)   Jo Ann Harmon, born May 16, 1930

        (3)   Frank Harold Harmon, born February 6, 1936

        (4)   Gail Deborah Harmon.

    c.   George Lucas Babington, Jr., born October 1, 1909, an infant death.

7.   Percy Edmond Thomas, born March 10, 1880, died January 26, 1904. Married 1903 to Leila Jackson.

8. Sallie Thomas, born c.1882, infant death.
9. Myrtie Lewis Thomas, born February 24, 1889 at Gaithersburg, Montgomery County, died April 2, 1967 at Cedar Grove, buried at Parklawn Cemetery, Rockville. Myrtie developed juvenile arthritis and was paralyzed for the last forty years of her life. Married at Rockville March 18, 1911 to Paul Meredith Slater, born January 25, 1884 in Loudoun County, Virginia and died October 5, 1968; son of James W. Slater and Mary Elizabeth Darr. A carpenter, he was buried at Potomac Methodist Church. Children:

a. Helen Virginia Slater, born January 7, 1912, died May 20, 1917 at Colesville, Maryland; buried at Potomac Methodist Church.

b. Grace Doris Slater, born October 11, 1915 at Ednor, Montgomery County. Married April 23, 1935 to Daniel Leonard Kraft, born June 1, 1911, died 1985 in Volusia County, Florida and had three children, born in Montgomery County, Maryland:

   (1) Mary Barbara Kraft, born May 30, 1936, and married November 1, 1954 in Madison County, Wisconsin to Julian Eugene Peters, born July 18, 1934 in Huntington, West Virginia, died January 18, 1992 in Volusia County, Florida; ashes spread at sea there off Atlantic coast.

   (2) Sharon Ann Kraft, born June 2, 1953; married April 6, 1985 in Maitland, Florida to Al Garan.

   (3) Pamela Gay Kraft, born January 9, 1958, and married January 16, 1988 John Murray Jones.

c. Mary Anna Slater, born June 1, 1917, of whom more.

d. Meredith Thomas Slater, born March 5, 1919 at Ednor. Married January 12, 1942 to Alice Myers, and had a son:

   (1) Thomas Gordon Slater, born September 20, 1944. Married August 21, 1966 to Margaret Ann Bean, born July 30, 1943 in Montgomery County, daughter of Harold Elsworth Bean and Martha Elizabeth Kidwell.

e. Robert Gordon Slater, born November 24, 1921 at Poolesville, died December 22, 1990. Married May 1,

1942 Margaret Mary Williams, born December 1, 1922.
Two children:

(1) William Robert Slater, born March 26, 1943 in Montgomery County, Maryland. Married to Kathy Keller, born 1943.

(2) Leslie Adele Slater, born March 19, 1947 in Livingston, Montana. Married 1969 Johnathan Muller, born February 14, 1947 at New Haven, Connecticut and divorced.

Mary Anna Slater
1917-1983

This daughter of Paul Meredith Slater (1884) and Myrtie Lewis Thomas (1889) was born June 1, 1917 at Ednor, Montgomery County, Maryland, died September 16, 1983 at Delta, Pennsylvania; buried with her husband at Parklawn Cemetery, Rockville. Married in Ellicott City August 10, 1934 to Joseph Leonard Beall, born April 23, 1913 at Rock Spring near Rockville, died February 1, 1971; son of William Leroy Beall and Nellie Edna Gill. Known by his middle name as Leonard Beall, he owned businesses in Rockville and later Cedar Grove. He was a talented singer, alone and in a quartet with his brothers. Five children, born in Montgomery County:

1. Janice Lee Beall, born August 6, 1938 at Takoma Park. Married August 26, 1954 in Arlington, Virginia to Lloyd Cecil Taylor, Jr., born April 22, 1934 at Bethesda, Maryland, son of Lloyd Cecil Taylor and Eva Rebecca Henley.

2. Kathleen Ann Beall, born March 8, 1942 at Takoma Park. Married October 9, 1960 in Rockville to Paul Richard King, born May 22, 1938 at Cedar Grove, the son of Leslie Crittenden King (1896) and Bertha Marie Beall (1901). Children:

    a. Peter Brandon King, born May 17, 1963. Married May 22, 1983 to Tracey Marie Copp, born July 3, 1963. They had children:

        (1) Krista Lyn King, born January 6, 1984
        (2) Josiah Brandon King, born July 29, 1996

b. David Andrew King, born March 13, 1966, and married November 26, 1994 to Susan Marie Hockenberry, born December 6, 1974. Children:
   (1) Amber Nichole King, born September 12, 1996
c. Leslie Lyn King, born October 28, 1968. Married August 20, 1988 Richard Wager Bailey, born July 24, 1964, and had children:
   (1) Richard Wager Bailey, Jr., born July 24, 1989
   (2) Christian Paul Bailey, born September 10, 1991
   (3) Luke Henry Bailey, born October 4, 1993
3. Marilyn Joy Beall, born November 17, 1944. Married Richard Ankney, born 1944, and divorced. Married second Richard A. Beck, born July 17, 1944 in Pennsylvania.
4. Mark Leonard Beall, born December 2, 1952 at Bethesda. Married to Janis Murphy, born November 22, 1952, daughter of Tom and Helen Murphy.
5. Mary Elizabeth Beall, born August 10, 1958 at Bethesda. Married first May 28, 1976 in Delta, Pennsylvania to Mark Reiller, born c.1957, divorced. Married second April 19, 1986 in Gaithersburg to Daniel Henkel, born December 5, 1954, son of Robert James and Ruth Henkel.

CHILD 6

George Thomas Trundle
1846-

This son of John Alexander Trundle (1813) and Elizabeth Eleanor Hays (1818) was born December 2, 1846. Married May 28, 1872 to Georgiana Lydia Moler, born January 18, 1852, died September 29, 1929; the daughter of Philip Rion Moler. Children:
1. John Alexander Trundle, born March 22, 1873 and married to Kittie Shepard, born March 2, 1881, died December 19, 1935. A daughter:
   a. Virginia Trundle, born November 4, 1904, married August 4, 1934 Paul Hauke, born March 8, 1903.
2. Willie May Trundle, born March 13, 1874 and died March 7, 1888

3. Daisy Florence Trundle, born April 14, 1875, died November 27, 1919
4. Lula M. Trundle, born May 19, 1876. Married January 17, 1900 to John Charles Burns, born May 16, 1876 and had at least three children:
   a. Jessie Clarence Burns, born November 9, 1900 and married February 8, 1922 to Maude V. Purdum, born November 9, 1900, daughter of James M. Purdum (1870) and Emma A. Davis (1873). A child:
      (1) Lula Virginia Burns, born April 16, 1923
   b. George Chapelle Burns, born March 7, 1903 and married March 28, 1926 to Scott Elaine McElveen.
   c. Georgia Louise Burns, born December 1, 1906, and married December 24, 1927 William Edward Hays, born c.1907, died December 8, 1960; buried at Forest Oak Cemetery, Gaithersburg. They had children:
      (1) Lulah Mae Hays, born March 4, 1930
      (2) Shirley Louise Hays, born July 14, 1934
      (3) Patricia Caywood Hays.
      (4) William Edward Hays, Jr.
5. Sarah Elizabeth Trundle, born 1878, died 1879
6. Beulah Whitaker Trundle, born January 7, 1881, died 1940. Married to Miller P. Moler, born July 25, 1882.
7. Samuel Rion Trundle, born February 14, 1883. Married October 11, 1905 Caroline Catherine Burns; children:
   a. George Burns Trundle, born September 19, 1906. Married to Mary E. Irvin.
   b. Samuel Rion Trundle, Jr., born January 2, 1910 and married 1933 to Lucy Ione Moler. A child:
      (1) Donald Edward Trundle, born October 7, 1935
   c. Dorothy Catherine Trundle, born June 17, 1935
8. George Thomas Trundle, Jr., born September 26, 1884. Married to Ida Christner. Two children:
   a. Miriam Amber Trundle, born January 22, 1910. Married to Robert Wackeman.
   b. Robert Christner Trundle, born December 3, 1913. Married to Edith L. Campbell.

9. Charles Moler Trundle, born May 14, 1886; married to Millie Burns, born August 18, 1886. Children:
   a. Mildred Trundle, born December 17, 1912, married c.1931 to Miller Webb and had children:
      (1) Joan Webb, born June 29, 1932
      (2) Charles Webb, born March 2, 1934
   b. Katherine Trundle, born November 6, 1919, married Norman Clevinger and had at least one child:
      (1) Norma Kay Clevinger.
   c. Doris Trundle, born November 6, 1922
   d. Joyce Trundle, born September 13, 1929
10. Mason Neel Trundle, born April 19, 1888, died November 2, 1930. Married first Fannie Mae Swomley, born May 26, 1891, died April 17, 1914, daughter of Calvin Grant Swomley and Annie Kate Kemp and had two children. Married second to Laura Whiltshire, born July, 1903, and had two children. We know one child from the first marriage, and the two from the second:
    a. George Neel Trundle, died at five months.
    b. Mary Louise Trundle, born December, 1922
    c. Emily Clarice Trundle, born November 24, 1928
11. Sarah Ann Trundle, born April 15, 1891; died that year.

CHILD 7

Harriet Abigail Trundle
1848-1928

This daughter of John Alexander Trundle (1813) and Elizabeth Eleanor Hays (1818) was born July 21, 1848, died August 7, 1928; buried at Mt. Olivet cemetery, in Frederick City. Married to David Dutrow Thomas, born April 11, 1845, died May 3, 1919; buried at Mt. Olivet. Children:
1. John Travers Thomas, born April 23, 1869. Married to Minnie L. Buckley and had three children:
   a. John Travers Thomas, Jr., born August 6, 1903, died May 25, 1905
   b. Mary Lorraine Thomas, married Donald J. Doub.

    c.   Caroline Buckey Thomas, married John W. Doub.

2.   David Dutrow Thomas, born February 16, 1871; married Elizabeth Williams and had five children:

    a.   David Dutrow Thomas, Jr., married Ruth Phillips and had children:

          (1) David Dutrow Thomas, 3rd.

          (2) James Phillips Thomas.

    b.   Elizabeth Thomas, married Edward Cecil Ritchie.

    c.   Helen Barton Thomas, married Page Selby:, and had at least one child

          (1) Helen Page Selby.

    d.   Margaret Williams Thomas.

    e.   Oscar Trundle Thomas, married Marion Lee Purcell

3.   Leona Thomas, born March 9, 1873; married to Howard L. Smith and had six children:

    a.   Helen Leona Smith.

    b.   Mary Ruth Smith, married Paul E. Soper. Children:

          (1) Harriet Elizabeth Soper.

          (2) Howard Kent Soper.

          (3) Eleanor Stuart Soper.

          (4) Cora W. Soper.

    c.   Howard Travers Smith, married Dorothy Zents and had children:

          (1) Dorothy Louise Smith.

          (2) Helen Lorraine Smith.

    d.   Harriet Elizabeth Smith, married Leonard E. Neale, Jr., and had children:

          (1) Leonard E. Neale, 3rd.

          (2) Sally Thomas Neale.

          (3) Mary Clara Neale.

    e.   Virginia Howard Smith, born 1902, died 1957. Married February 19, 1924 to Josiah Brandenburg, born 1894, died 1972, son of Theodore McAuley Brandenburg (1855) and Amanda Catherine Harp (1857), and had at least a daughter:

(1) Virginia Ann Brandenburg, born August 24, 1925. Married November 29, 1947 to Thomas Eugene Walsh. Six children.

    f. Bernard Thomas Smith.

4. Charlotte Elizabeth Thomas, born July 1, 1876. Married Gerry Lakin and had a daughter:

    a. Alberta Trundle Lakin, married Oliver C. Hall.

5. Bernard O. Thomas, a twin, a doctor, born November 6, 1882. Married Margaret L. Bartholow and had children:

    a. Bernard O. Thomas.

    b. James Barthalow Thomas.

6. Oscar E. Thomas, a twin, born November 6, 1882. Married Josephine Rundollar and had children:

    a. Edward O. Thomas.

    b. Mary Josephine Thomas.

CHILD 9

Laura Virginia Trundle
1851-1927

This daughter of John Alexander Trundle (1813) and Elizabeth Eleanor Hays (1818) was born April 5, 1851 in Frederick County, died July 31, 1927. She was married January 16, 1872 to Charles Thomas Brosius, born October 1, 1847 in Frederick County, died December 15, 1923 at Barnesville, in Montgomery County; son of John S. Brosius and Margaret Maria Shafer. The family was listed in the 1900 census for the Eleventh District of Montgomery County, which stated that Charles and Laura had been married 28 years, and had nine children, all then living. Children:

1. Anne Alonnie Brosius, born August 14, 1874, died December 18, 1950. Married June 25, 1902 to Claggett C. Hilton, born February 24, 1867, died January 14, 1933, son of William T. Hilton and Rebecca Snyder. A son:

    a. William Brosius Hilton, born April 26, 1903, died February 24, 1977; buried at Monocacy. Director of Hilton Funeral Home, Barnesville. Married November 28, 1928 in Washington to Sarah Constance Chiswell, born April 3, 1906, died October 7, 1982 in Frederick; buried at Monocacy; the daughter of Lawrence Allnutt Chiswell (1869) and Harriett Maguire Hersberger (1874). A son:

    (1) William Hilton.

2. Margaret Virginia Brosius, born October 6, 1876, died October 2, 1961 at Dickerson, Maryland. Married June 12, 1909 to Reginald Bernard Jones, born June 13, 1877, died October 2, 1961; buried at St. Mary's Cemetery, Barnesville, Maryland, with his wife. He was a son of Henry Robert Jones and Mary Eloise Scholl. Children:

    a. Reginald Bernard Jones, Jr., born June 15, 1910 at Dickerson, died January 29, 1988. Married August 23, 1935 to Helen Jennison, born January 9, 1917 in Chevy Chase, Maryland, died October 15, 1988 in Hong Kong, China; daughter of Clay Jennison and Meryl Greenman. Six children, including:

        (1) Reginald Bernard Jones, 3rd.

        (2) Richard Lawrence Jones.

    b. Margaret Virginia Jones, born December 16, 1913, died July 16, 1950 at home, Dickerson, Maryland; buried St. Mary's Cemetery at Barnesville. Married first November 30, 1933 to Bernard Hopkins Thomas, born June 1, 1912 and had a son. Married second William Thomas Kessler.

    c. Charles Robert Jones, born January 28, 1918. Married October 16, 1938 to Reva Eloise Alexander, born October 9, 1918, daughter of John H. Alexander and Susan Hester Hawker. At least a child:

        (1) Joan Temple Jones.

3. Charles Thomas Brosius, Jr., born March 27, 1879, died April 19, 1938 at Lime Kiln, Maryland; buried at Monocacy cemetery. Married November 4, 1908 to Genevieve Mattingly Darby, born February 23, 1888, died June 16, 1970 at Silver Spring, Maryland; buried at Monocacy; daughter of Remus Riggs Darby (1847) and Antoinette Griffith Chiswell (1858). Four children:

    a. Antoinette Grove Brosius, born August 2, 1909

b. Virginia Brosius, born February 23, 1912. Married July 16, 1932 to George L. Thomas, Jr. Children:
   (1) George L. Thomas, 3rd: April 27, 1934
   (2) Charles Brosius Thomas, born September 19, 1935.
c. Charles Thomas Brosius, 3rd, born November 20, 1916. Married Ellen Ayers.
d. Dorothy Brosius, born December 3, 1922

4. Elizabeth Eleanor Brosius, born September 30, 1881, died July 7, 1952 in Frederick; buried at St. Mary's Cemetery in Barnesville. Married November 23, 1904 to Lloyd James Jones, born November 19, 1878, died October 18, 1954; buried at St. Mary's; son of E. S. Mercer Jones (1848) and Sarah Elizabeth Trundle (1843). Three children:
   a. R. Elizabeth Jones, born October 26, 1905
   b. Mary Virginia Jones, born August 7, 1906, married July 14, 1931 to Irvin Fisk and had a daughter:
      (1) Mary Virginia Fisk, born March 2, 1933
      (2) Lawrence Irvin Fisk.
   c. Lloyd James Jones, Jr., born May 12, 1911, married to Louise Hersperger.

5. John William Brosius, born November 14, 1884, died June 18, 1945; buried at Monocacy. Married April 5, 1910 to Louise Pearre Davis, born May 10, 1886, died October 19, 1968; the daughter of T. Wallace Davis. Children:
   a. John William Brosius, Jr., born November 7, 1919. Married first September 6, 1945 Merle A. Fair, born in Sydney, Australia, and had three children. Married second in 1945 Alicia Duarte. Known as Bill, he and brother Louie (next) were well-known builders in both Frederick and Montgomery Counties, operating as Brosius Brothers, and achieved national attention with the introduction of their largest project, *Lake Linganore,* in Frederick Co.
   b. Louie Brosius, born August 27, 1922 at Adamstown, Maryland. Served in the Marines in World War 2; married Angie Feire and had four children (see above also).
   c. Viola Brosius.
   d. Minnie Brosius.

6. Mary Loretta Brosius, born March 23, 1886, died April 19, 1968. Married February 15, 1910 to Notley Hays Davis, born December 19, 1883, died June 1, 1953 at Barnesville; buried at Monocacy, son of John Wallace Davis (1854) and Harriet Abigail Hays (1860). Three children:
   a. Mary Loretta Davis, born November 18, 1911 and married May 29, 1934 to Leonard Jerome Offutt, born June 7, 1910. A son:
      (1) Leonard Jerome Offutt, Jr., born April 26, 1935
   b. Laura Virginia Davis, born December 1, 1914
   c. Notley Hays Davis, Jr., born February 16, 1919
7. Leonard Jarboe Brosius, born July 23, 1888, died March 14, 1910.
8. Edward Rawlins Brosius, born May 5, 1891, died 1974. Married August 2, 1916 to Bertha Adell Schaeffer at her home in Seneca, Maryland, born June 19, 1896, died 1964, daughter of William L. Schaeffer. Four children:
   a. Edward Rawlins Brosius, Jr., born June 21, 1918
   b. Bertram S. Brosius, born June 10, 1921
   c. Catherine Alonnie Brosius, born December 27, 1925
   d. Margaret Cecelia Brosius, born June 1, 1927
9. Bernard Trundle Brosius, born February 23, 1893, died February 2, 1955 in Howard County, Maryland; buried St. Mary's Cemetery, Barnesville, Montgomery County. Married first January 24, 1924 to Dorothy Virginia Gott, born October 1, 1903, died January 14, 1968, daughter of James Perry Gott and Lillian Pearl Atwell; divorced after one daughter:
   a. Joan Brosius, born January 9, 1930

CHILD 10

Sarah John Trundle
1853-1925

This daughter of John Alexander Trundle (1813) and Elizabeth Eleanor Hays (1818) was born December 2, 1853, died January 22, 1925. Married June 3, 1884 to James T. Kramer, born November 11, 1843, died September 5, 1885. A child:

1. Hester Trundle Kramer, born April 30, 1885 and married September 6, 1914 to Brenton A. Devol, born March 22, 1882, and had children:
   a. Sarah John Devol, born March 11, 1916
   b. Brenton A. Devol, Jr., born July 31, 1917
   c. James Thomas Kramer Devol, born August 8, 1919
   d. Mary Jane Devol, born May 16, 1923

CHAPTER 4

Miscellaneous Hays Family Members

Montgomery County, Maryland

In the course of research, a number of references have been found in Montgomery County records to various members of the Hays families, who have yet to be identified within any of the family groups discussed in the previous chapters. They are presented here for further study.

Frank R. Hayes

Identified in the obituary of his wife, Frank was married to Alice M., born c.1819, and died October 22, 1994 at Suburban Hospital, Bethesda, Montgomery County, Maryland; buried at Parklawn Cemetery. Survived by her husband and four children:
1. Marilyn Hayes, married to Chmieleweski.
2. Carol A. Hayes, married to Simpson.
3. Douglas P. Hayes.
4. Mark A. Hayes.

Franklyn O. Hayes
died 1980

The obituary of Mary Hayes, born c.1916, died December 21, 1999, stated that she was born in Newport News, Virginia, died at Phoenix, Arizona; but had lived much of her life in Rockville. She was survived by four sons:
1. David Hayes, of Phoenix.
2. Richard Hayes, of Colorado Springs, Colorado.
3. Douglas Hayes, of Laurel, Maryland.
4. Paul Hayes, of Leesburg, Virginia.

A number of miscellaneous small bits of information were also found, listed following. All the individuals in the left column bear

55

the Hays surname by birth or by marriage. All events occurred in Montgomery County, Maryland, unless otherwise noted.

Individual	Event
Angus	Md Margaret Ruth Poole, d/o Warner Seymore Poole and Ella Independence Orme (1864) and had children: Edward and Catherine Hays.
David E., Jr.	Born 08/26/1921, died 01/21/1975.
Edward L.	Md 11/18/1880 to Anna T. Waring in Washington, D. C.
Howard B.	Born 1912, died 1972; buried at the Rockville cemetery.
Leonard John Odel	Born 02/05/1842, son of William and Eleanor. Records of St. Peter's Church, Poolesville.
Linwood J.	Md 10/03/1906 to Mary Eloise Gott, who was born 02/04/1887, died 07/26/1955 d/o Benjamin Nathan Gott (1856) and Anna Mary Scholl (1859), and had six children. Mary Eloise was apparently married second to Millard, and is buried at Monocacy in the Benjamin J. Hays plot, who may be her son. Buried there also are: Thomas Preston Hays, born 01/20/1910, died 11/25/1981, CBM, USNavy, WWII; and Mary E. (Hays) Hardy, born 06/06/1927, and died 10/05/1956; who may be two more children of Linwood and Mary Eloise.
Martha A.	Born 08/11/1856, d/o S. R. and S. A. Hays.
Wilford E.	Born 12/26/1923, died 11/25/1977; buried at Potomac Methodist Cemetery. Wife Helen S., born 12/31/1923.

Frederick County, Maryland

Most early families in the northwestern sections of Montgomery County had family members living in Frederick County at some point in time. From 1748 to 1776, all of Montgomery was a part of Frederick and records during that period must be checked in the parent county. Even to this day, the older families in that area of Montgomery are more oriented toward Frederick than Rockville for their day-to-day needs, medical and legal matters. In any case, the Hays family was no exception, and a number of references have been found to families there, as here reported. A few references used the surname spelling Hayes, but more often Hays, which we will use throughout this report.

Jonathan Hays, Jr.

References to this individual were found in *History of Frederick County, Maryland,* by T. J. C. Williams, 1910, reprinted 1997 for Clearfield Company. He was a son of an older Jonathan Hayes and Elizabeth Elliott. The first Jonathan was said to be of England, and was an officer in the British Army stationed at Philadelphia (or Elizabethtown, as it was originally known). He resigned his commission in order to marry Elizabeth, who was a Quaker, settled in Delaware, and raised a large family, including twelve sons, of which Jonathan, Jr. was one.

As a young man, Jonathan Hays, Jr. relocated to Baltimore and then to an area along Tom's Creek above its mouth on the Monocacy River in what was later to become Frederick County, obtaining a patent for land about 1739. It is said that one of his favorite brothers, Samuel, once visited him at the farm and Jonathan offered to give him one hundred acres if he would remain, which was accepted. The tract was surveyed off and appropriately called *Brotherly Love.*

Jonathan, Jr. was reportedly married to a Miss Henderson, and had three sons and two daughters, born in Frederick County. He is said to be buried there on the old farm. The children, not necessarily in birth order, were:
1. Jahue Hays, relocated to southern Virginia.
2. John Hays, relocated to Tennessee, married Miss Coffee, returned for a time to his father's farm, and went back to Tennessee. He had at least one son:
    a. John Coffee Hayes, better known as General Hayes of Texas Ranger fame, intrepid Indian fighter, and served under General Scott in Mexico. When California became

part of the United States, "brave Jack Coffee Hayes" was selected to become Sheriff of San Francisco County, and charged with enforcement of law in the new territory, rising to the rank of Colonel; after which he was appointed by President Pierce to become surveyor general of the state of California.

3. Joseph Hays, married Deborah Weimer, the only daughter of Joseph Weimer of Taneytown, and had four sons and three daughters:
    a. Abraham W. Hays, born c.1794, died December 4, 1836. Served from August to October, 1814 under Captain William Knox during the War of 1812. Married c.1826 to Henrietta Musgrave, born c.1795, died July 10, 1837. Both buried in the old cemetery at Taneytown.
    b. Thomas Hays, born c.1791, of whom more following.
    c. Joseph Hays, Jr., married Miss Fuss.
    d. John Hays, married Miss Frame.
    e. Elizabeth Elliott Hays, married Phillip Hahn.
    f. Mary Hays, married John Pomeroy.
    g. Deborah Weimer Hays, single.

4. Daughter Hays, married to Thomas Wilson.

5. Daughter Hays, married to John Smith, who farmed near Emmitsburg, and had four sons and four daughters.

Thomas Hays
1791-1843

This son of Joseph Hays and Deborah Weimer was born c.1791, died July 10, 1843, and is buried at the Emmitsburg Presbyterian Church in Frederick County. His wife and two sons are buried with him. She was Elizabeth Armstrong, born c.1798, died July 5, 1850, daughter of John Armstrong, Jr., a gun-maker of Emmitsburg. Elizabeth was head of household in the 1850 census of Frederick County, in the Borough of Emmitsburg, a widow, with three children at home. Living with her was Catharine Wetsel, born c.1832, not otherwise identified. The children were all born on the hill opposite St. Joseph's Church in Emmitsburg, the house being the first to burn in the great Emmitsburg fire of 1863. Children:

1. John Thomas Hays, born c.1826, died September 29, 1827 and buried with his parents.
2. William Hays, married Sarah Nickum.
3. Joseph Hays, born c.1829, a millwright. He is perhaps the same Joseph who was born August 13, 1828, died December 5, 1888, and is buried at the Emmitsburg Presbyterian Church with his wife, Elizabeth Curren, born July 1, 1823, died April 30, 1863, daughter of William and Jane Curren. They were married January 18, 1853 in Frederick County. Three children are buried with them:
   a. Andrew T. Hays, a minister, born December 22, 1856, died November 23, 1886.
   b. Willie VanLear Hays, born Mary 14, 1859, died September 11, 1866.
   c. Elizabeth Hays, born September 1, 1861, died August 30, 1863.
4. John Hays, born c.1831 (or 1841), died June 4, 1837 (or 1847) at the age of six years; buried with his parents.
5. James Thomas Hays, born March 31, 1833, died March 18, 1912; buried at Emmitsburg Presbyterian Church with his wife. Married in Frederick County December 27, 1858 Sarah Ann Witherow, born January 22, 1832, died April 1, 1912. Formed a partnership with his brother Joseph, known as J. and J. T. Hays. They later bought the Emmitsburg foundry in 1856. James and Sarah had two sons and two daughters:
   a. John Witherow Hays, born March 18, 1865, died April 25, 1866, buried with his parents.
   b. Thomas C. Hays, born October 3, 1862, died May 9, 1934; buried with his wife at Mountain View cemetery, Emmitsburg. Married to Minnie E. Fox,, born August 9, 1872, died November 5, 1955 and had five sons and a daughter:
      (1) James T. Hays.
      (2) William E. Hays.
      (3) John Ross Hays.
      (4) Samuel C. Hays.
      (5) Harry W. Hays.
      (6) Sarah Margaret Hays.

c. Lizzie Ross Hays, married to E. D. Snively of Greencastle, Pennsylvania. Two children:
   (1) Mary Snively.
   (2) Isabelle Snively.
d. Sarah Weimer Hays.
6. Samuel Elliott Hays, born c.1836 married a Miss Dennis of Texas, and was an attorney at law.
7. Deborah Weimer Hays, married Darius Thomas and moved to Iowa.

Levin Hays
1803-

Head of household in the 1850 census of Frederick County, in the Tenth Election District, Levin was born c.1803. He had a wife Julia Anne, born c.1803, died March 2, 1876; buried at Wolfsville Lutheran Church, and there were seven children:
1. John Hays, born c.1828
2. Harriet Hays, born c.1834
3. Allen Hays, born January 31, 1836, died November 11, 1919. Buried at Wolfsville Lutheran Church. Wife Martha A. S., born c.1848, died July 22, 1875; buried at Ellerton Brethren Church. Allen was apparently married a second time after the death of Martha. He was found as head of household in the 1880 census of the Catoctin District, with Lydia Hays, born c.1848, listed as wife. She died October 14, 1937 and is buried with her husband. Living with him was his father Levin, listed as a shoemaker. There were four children at home:
   a. Ola Hays, born c.1869
   b. Minnie Hays, born c.1873
   c. Lude Hays, a daughter, born c.1877
   d. Milton U. Hays, born c.1878
4. Henry C. Hays, born c.1838, died February 22, 1908; buried at Mt. Bethel Methodist Church, Garfield, with his wife and two children. His wife was Susan C., born c.1849, died November 6, 1925. There may have been others, but the two children buried with there parents were:
   a. Rutherford Hays, born c.1877, died May 17, 1877

b. Mark A. Hays, born c.1881, died February 22, 1900
5. Susan E. Hays, born c.1841, died November 16, 1851; buried at Wolfsville with her mother.
6. Amanda M. Hays, born c.1843
7. Denton C. Hays, born c.1846

Catharine Hays
1805-

Head of household in the 1850 census of Frederick County, in the Petersville District, Catharine was born c.1805 in Maryland, and was listed as a pauper, apparently widowed. There were two children living with her, apparently hers:
1. George W. Hays, born c.1838
2. William F. Hays, born c.1840

Joseph Hays
1806-

Head of household in the 1850 census of Frederick County, in the Creagerstown District, Joseph was born c.1806 in Maryland and was a blacksmith. He was apparently widowed, with four children at home. Living in the household was Elizabeth Haam, born c.1800 not otherwise identified. The children were:
1. Daniel Hays, born c.1834
2. Debra Hays, born c.1837
3. Joseph Hays, born c.1839
4. Thomas Hays, born c.1843

Keturah Hays
1799-

Head of household in the 1850 census of Frederick County, in Frederick Town, Keturah was born c.1799, and was apparently a widow, with four daughters at home. Living in the household was Julian Hays, a female, born c.1798, not otherwise identified. This may be the same as Julia Ann Hayes, born July 28, 1794, died March 26, 1860; buried at Mt. Olivet Cemetery. In 1850, Keturah also owned one twelve-year old female slave. Records of Mt. Olivet Cemetery, Frederick, report the burial of Keturah, died October 26, 1864 at the age of 66 years. The children were:

1. Elizabeth A. Hays, born c.1826, died December 11, 1851 and buried at Mt. Olivet Cemetery in Frederick with her mother. The report of her death includes "of W. H." referring apparently to her father.
2. Sarah E. Hays, born c.1831
3. Josephine H. Hays, born c.1834
4. Maria L. Hays, born c.1838

William Hays
1785-

Head of household in the 1850 census of Frederick County, in the Catoctin District, William was born c.1785 in Maryland, and was a merchant. His wife was Mary, born c.1780, and they then had what appeared to be a son at home, and perhaps a grandson, William Hays, born c.1843. The apparent son was:

1. Wilson L. Hays, born c.1817, a salesman.

Harrison Hayes
1841-

Head of household in the 1880 census of Catoctin District, Harrison was a collier, with a wife Sarah, born c.1844, and six children at home:

1. Wesley Hayes, born c.1867
2. Louisa E. Hayes, born c.1871
3. Melinda Hayes, born c.1874
4. James C. Hayes, born c.1876
5. Sarah Hayes, a twin, born c.1879
6. Temmie Hayes, a twin, born c.1879

John O. Hays
1829-

Head of household in the 1880 census of the Catoctin District of Frederick County, John was born c.1829, and was a school teacher. His wife was Sophia Fox, born c.1831, daughter of George P. Fox and Sophia Bussard, and there were three children at home. Based on the age differences between the children it is possible that the marriage to Sophia was his second; or that there had been several children not at home as of 1880. Children:

1. Ellen Hays, born c.1858
2. Unnamed son, born c.1872
3. Albert O. Hays, born c.1874

In the course of research, a number of individual "one-liner" bits of information were found relative to family members. All the individuals in the left column bear the Hays surname by birth or by marriage. All events occurred in Frederick County, Maryland, unless otherwise noted.

NOTE

There are numerous entries for Hays family members listed in *Names In Stone*, Volume 1, by Jacob Mehrling Holdcraft who have not been identified, and are not copied here; please refer to that reference. Similarly, the researcher should check *Marriage Licenses of Frederick County*, in three volumes: 1778-1810; 1811-1840; and 1841-1865, by Margaret E. Myers, which also contain numerous references not yet identified, and not included here.

Individual	Event
Arthur	Born c.1837 in Maryland; in 1850 a student at Mount Saint Mary's College.
Catharine A.	Born c.1819, died during March, 1850 in the Catoctin District of Frederick County.
Charles	Born c.1836 in Maryland; in 1850 census of Creagerstown District, Frederick County, living in household of Henry Black (1814).
George H.	Born c.1829; in the 1850 census of Frederick Town, he was listed as a hatter, in the house-

	hold of Washington James (1806), who was a cigar maker.
Goodlow	Born c.1817; in the 1850 census of Catoctin District, listed as a cooper, living in household of Joseph Stottlemeyer (1801), a farmer.
James	Born c.1831 in Maryland; in the 1850 census of Creagerstown District, listed as a millwright, living in household of Daniel Wireman (1790), also a millwright, as were four other individuals in that household.
Josiah	Born c.1849; in the 1850 census of Catoctin District, living in the household of Mary Gaver (1799).
M. R.	Female, born c.1825; in 1850 census of the 5th District, a Sister of Charity, St. Joseph's.
Mary M.	Born c.1847; in the 1850 census of Middletown District, living in household of Hezekiah Poffenberger (1828), a blacksmith.
Sarah A.	Born c.1842; in the 1850 census of Woodsboro District, living in household of Daniel Root of R. (1806).
Susan R.	Born c.1843; in the 1850 census of Catoctin District, living in household of Rebecca Easterday (1800).
Wilson	Born c.1786, died 05/15/1856; buried at the Wolfsville Lutheran Church. Wife Mary, born c.1776, died 08/28/1853; buried Brandenburg Family cemetery, Wolfsville.

Washington County, Maryland

As noted elsewhere in the text, a few members of the Hays families Montgomery County moved to Washington County during the early years. They would have found other families bearing that same surname, but apparently from a different line of descent. One such family was that of Wilson Hays.

Wilson Lee Hays, Jr.
1820-1889

A biography of one of the members of this family appeared in *History of Washington County, Maryland*, Volume 2, by Thomas J. C. Williams, originally published in 1906, and most recently in 1992 for Clearfield Publishing Company. The father of Wilson Hays, Jr. was born in Scotland, and emigrated to the United States, apparently at about the end of the eighteenth century. He had at least one son, our subject, and perhaps other children as well. The one son with whom we here deal was:

1. Wilson Lee Hays, Jr., born c.1820 in Frederick County, Maryland, and died c.1889, probably in Hagerstown, Maryland. Married in Frederick County by license dated November 11, 1850 to Susanna Recher of that county. The family moved to Hagerstown, in Washington County, about 1866, and Wilson became associated with the Hagerstown Sash Factory. He and Susanna were parents of at least four sons:

    a. Rufus M. Hays, apparently the founder of the business firm, R. M. Hays and Brothers in Hagerstown, which included his brothers Chester and Ira as partners.

    b. Leroy Hays, who relocated to Philadelphia.

    c. Chester R. Hays.

    d. Ira W. Hays, born September 17, 1855 at Wolfsville, in Frederick County. Between 1874 and 1876, Ira was employed as a printer with the Government Printing Office in Washington. Returning to Hagerstown, he established a job printing business, and in 1879, founded the *Hagerstown Globe*, a daily and weekly newspaper of Washington County, which he owned and published. Married May 21, 1879 to Flora V. Householder, daughter of William Householder of Hagerstown, and had four children, three of whom survived:

        (1) J. Clyde Hays.

        (2) Clifford E. Hays.

        (3) Vernie V. Hays.

CHAPTER 5

Richard Gott
died c.1661

The earliest known ancestor of the Gott families of Montgomery County, Maryland, Richard is reported to have transported himself, his wife, two children, and four servants to Anne Arundel County in 1650, the year of the county's formation on the west side of the Chesapeake Bay. There is no indication that he was of noble descent, nor of his country of origin, although he was probably born in England, perhaps in Yorkshire or Lincolnshire, where the name is reasonably common. The Maryland Historical Society in Baltimore reportedly holds a descendency chart of the family prepared by Christopher Johnston, from which some of the following was derived.

It is possible that Richard was first an indentured servant in Virginia, and moved to Maryland after having first completed that service, as other Virginians had, claiming the land grants offered as a condition of settlement. At the time of his arrival in Maryland, he was entitled to one hundred acres for himself, one hundred for his wife, and fifty acres for each child and each servant transported. In 1659, the 600-acre tract called Ram Gott Swamp was surveyed for Richard Gott, located on the west side of Chesapeake Bay and the north side of Herring Creek (known today as Tracey's Creek. The present-day town of Deale, Maryland, is located on the original Gott patent.

Richard was in Maryland as early as 1650, bringing with him his wife Susan, whose surname is not known. He died there before February, 1661, when records discuss the settlement of his estate. Richard left a will dated November 28, 1660, probated February 20, 1662, naming his wife, his only son, and daughter Susan who were born in Maryland. Neither of the two who arrived with their parents were mentioned. After the death of her husband, Susan was married secondly to Henry Hooper. Children of Richard and Susan:

1. Sarah Gott, arrived with her parents in Anne Arundel County in 1650. Married there first to Alexander Gordon, to whom

Richard assigned the indenture of Edward Parrish in 1659, as well as two hundred acres of land, perhaps as the dowry of his daughter. They had no children. She was married second to John Ewen, who died c.1669, without children. Sarah married third Robert Franklin, who died c.1682; one child. Married fourth to John Willoughby, who died c.1702; no children. The one child was:

    a.   Sarah Franklin.

2.   Juliatha Gott, arrived with her parents in Anne Arundel County in 1650.

3.   Richard Gott, born between 1650 when his parents arrived in Maryland, and 1660, the date of his father's will, assumed to be c.1653 for purposes of presentation here, and of whom more following.

4.   Susan Gott, born between 1650 when her parents arrived in Maryland, and 1660, the date of her father's will.

Richard Gott
1653-1715

This son of the immigrant Richard Gott (died c.1661) and his wife Susan, was born about 1653, probably in Herring Creek Hundred, Anne Arundel County. He was married twice, first to Hannah Pratt, who died between 1688 and 1691, daughter of Thomas Pratt, who left a will dated August 14, 1686, in which he named his daughter Hannah, and his son-in-law Richard Gott. There were two children born to Richard and Hannah. Richard was married second to Elizabeth Holland, born c.1673, died c.1718, daughter of Anthony Holland, who died in Anne Arundel County c.1703. He left a will dated February 12, 1702 and probated August 2, 1703 in which he described four tracts of land that he had lying in Herring Creek Swamp, being 120 acres of Goldsborough, 50 acres of the *Great Neck*, 120 acres of *Holland's Range*, and 18 acres of *Locust Neck*. In his will, Anthony Holland does not mention a wife, but names ten children to receive various bequests from the estate. To his daughter Eliza, wife of Richard Gott, Herring Creek, he left 100 acres of *Holland's Choice*, which was a 580-acre tract located in Baltimore County.

Richard Gott of 1653 also left a will in Anne Arundel County, dated December 28, 1713, and probated April 16, 1715. That will is one of the more important documents relative to this family, in that he names his children, with their attained ages at the time of making the will. He does not name his wife, although he refers to her one-third portion as a reservation from other bequests. He names as his Executor son-in-law John Cheshire, who later relinquished his rights of administration to the widow and her second husband. After Richard's death, his widow Elizabeth married secondly to Thomas Woodfield. The first two listed children were born to the first marriage of Richard Gott; the remainder to the second, all in Anne Arundel County, Maryland:

1. Hannah Gott, born June 29, 1686; married July 18, 1706 to John Cheshire.

2. Susanna Gott, born June 29, 1688; married July 10, 1711 to Abel Hill. He left a will in Anne Arundel County dated February 28, 1758, which did not name a wife, who perhaps predeceased him. He named several grandchildren and children:
   a. Susannah Hill, married to Dowell.
   b. Hesther Hill, married to Richard Weems.
   c. Abel Hill, Jr., married and had children, including:
      (1) Abel Hill, III.
   d. Sarah Hill, married to Cambden.
   e. Joseph Hill.

3. Richard Gott, born May 2, 1692, died in Baltimore County. Married to Sarah, and in 1737 leased a part of *Gunpowder Manor* called *Dublin*, to run for the lifetimes of his children Elizabeth and Richard, Jr. Richard Gott, Planter, left a will dated March 24, 1742 in Baltimore County, proven June 4, 1751. He names his wife Sarah, and leaves his lands to sons Samuel, Richard and Anthony, with the provision that no division or payment be made to any of his seven children (other than the three sons first named) until two years after his death, and that his "dear wife" be not deprived of the use of their part until that time. Note that the last three children have no birth dates, and perhaps would fill in between some of the missing years. Children, not necessarily in this birth order:

a. Ruth Gott, born February 9, 1715, married to William Towson.
b. Samuel Gott, born May 10, 1718, died c.1787, leaving a will dated February 23, 1787, probated April 9, 1787. Married to Rachel, who was perhaps Rachel Norwood, daughter of Edward Norwood. They had children:
   (1) Edward Gott.
   (2) Richard Gott.
   (3) Ann Gott, married Bosley.
   (4) Rachel Gott, married Stansbury and had children:
       (a) Rachel Stansbury.
       (b) Susanna Stansbury.
   (5) Sarah Gott, married Perine.
   (6) Elizabeth Gott.
   (7) Susanna Gott, married Hunt.
c. Sarah Gott, born January 19, 1722, died c.1759. Married to Stephen Hart Owings at Baltimore, who died there c.1801, and had children, born at Baltimore:
   (1) Sarah Owings, born March 19, 1742
   (2) Richard Gott Owings, born January 18, 1743, died January, 1806. Married to Ruth, who died February 1, 1836 and had children, born in Baltimore:
       (a) Joshua Owings.
       (b) Stephen Owings.
       (c) Nicholas Owings, born c.1772, died c.1851. Married May 20, 1814 at Zanesville, Ohio to Margaret Conn.
       (d) Elizabeth Owings, born c.1773, married September 26, 1795 at Baltimore Thomas Cockey.
       (e) Beal Owings, born November 22, 1785, married to Henrietta Butler.
       (f) Richard Owings, born c.1789, died April 24, 1855 in Baltimore County. Married there June 15, 1811 to Nancy Fishbaugh.
       (g) Thomas Owings, born c.1791
       (h) Samuel Owings, born c.1793
       (i) Essah Owings, born c.1795
   (3) Caleb Owings, died December 23, 1795

(4) Samuel Owings, born March 12, 1747; married to Marcy Turner.

(5) Stephen Hart Owings, Jr., born June 24, 1750

(6) Cassandra Owings, born c.1752

(7) Nicholas Owings, born September 30, 1755

(8) Hannah Owings, born c.1757

(9) Beal Owings, born c.1759

d. Elizabeth Gott, born May 11, 1724

e. Richard Gott, Jr., born May 15, 1726 in Baltimore. Married there April 30, 1758 to Ruth Bond, daughter of Richard Bond. By 1750, he owned 400 acres of *Gott's Hope* and 100 acres of *Addition to Gott's Hope*. He left a will, dated June 14, 1793, naming his wife and children:

(1) Elizabeth Gott, born January 22, 1759

(2) Eleanor Gott, born June 21, 1760

(3) Richard Gott, born January 6, 1761

(4) Mary Gott, born March 30, 1764

(5) Hannah Gott, married to Woods.

(6) Ruth Gott.

(7) Achsah Gott.

f. Cassandra Gott, born August 1, 1728

g. Anthony Gott, born March 19, 1731. He is perhaps the same Anthony who was married to Sarah Owings and had at least two sons, born in Baltimore County:

(1) Samuel H. Gott, born c.1773, married to Rebecca Haile and had children:

(a) William Gott, an early death.

(b) Richard H. Gott.

(c) Claiborn Gott, born c.1808

(d) Nancy Gott, born c.1812

(e) Alfred Gott, born c.1813

(2) Lott O. Gott, born c.1776, died in Sullivan County, Tennessee. Married there Elizabeth Perry, daughter of David Perry. Children:

(a) Elizabeth Gott, born April 6, 1798, died August 17, 1869

(b) Roland Perry Gott, born May 5, 1802, died September 17, 1874. Married to Rachel H. Childress.

(c) Sarah Gott, born c.1803, died February 21, 1884

(d) John G. Gott, born April 8, 1806, died February 23, 1881

(e) Hannah Gott, born c.1808

(f) Mary Gott, born January 11, 1809, died May 27, 1872

(g) Elkana Gott, born c.1812

(h) Ruth Gott, born c.1814, died February 19, 1841

(i) David Gott, born c.1815

(j) Harvey Gott, born c.1821, died March 20, 1849

(k) Jesse Gott, born April 22, 1822, died February 7, 1908

(l) Eliza Jane Gott, born c.1823

(m) William Gott, born c.1829

h. Hannah Gott.

i. Susanna Gott.

j. Rachel Gott.

4. Robert Gott, born May 2, 1693, died about August, 1754. Robert was married to Elizabeth Walters, and left a will in Anne Arundel County dated April 9, 1754, probated September 3, 1754, in which he names his wife and his children. There were first three specific bequests of one slave each to three of his sons, and then the balance of the estate divided between the children. Prerogative Court records dated March 16, 1759 relative to the estate of Robert Gott name next of kin as Joseph Gott and Anthony Gott; Executor was William Gott. Children:

a. Ezekiel Gott, born c.1735, and received one slave, and of whom more following.

b. John Gott, who received one slave.

c. Samuel Gott, who received one slave.

d. Walter Gott.

e. Verlinda Gott.

f. William Gott.

5. Anthony Gott, born September 15, 1694, who received the "land sold to father-in-law Anthony Holland, but which came to testator again by right of wife," and of whom more in Chapter 2.

6. Matthew Gott, born July 31, 1697.

7. John Gott, born c.1700, who received one half of the plantation, reserving the wife's one third; provided that should he die without issue, brother Matthew is to inherit his share. Married first about 1727 to Esther Crandall, daughter of Francis Crandall and Esther Hill. The will of Francis Crandall, probated in Anne Arundel County November 30, 1744 names Esther Gott as one his daughters.

8. Sarah Gott, born c.1704; married July 23, 1726 to Thomas Metcalf.

9. Samuel Gott, born March 7, 1706, who received the residue of the dwelling plantation, provided that should he die without issue, brother Robert is to inherit his share. Died about 1715.

10. Capell Gott, a son, born September 27, 1709. Died before 1733, single.

Ezekiel Gott
1735-

This son of Robert Gott (1693) and Elizabeth Walters was born c.1735 in Anne Arundel County, Maryland. Married November 12, 1761 to Elizabeth Soper and had children, including:

1. Ezekiel Gott, born December 1, 1761 on Allendale Farm in Anne Arundel County, and died there April 7, 1801. Married at St. James Church in Lothian, Anne Arundel, April 23, 1792 to Susanna Jackson Soper, who died c.1845 on Allendale Farm. She was a daughter of Nathan Soper (1762) of Prince George's County. Nathan Soper left a will dated April 4, 1817 is found in Liber TT at folio 353 in Prince George's County, and entered March 24, 1824. There, he leaves to his three daughters, Susanna J. Gott, Eleanor Childs, and Martha Beale, all his lands in Washington County, Maryland. Settle-

ment of his estate during the July Term of 1828 appears in Chancery Records of the county, filed in Liber B-137 at folio 644 at the Hall of Records in Annapolis. The property in Washington County is part of the tract of land known as *Soper's Purchase*, containing 455 and a quarter acres, to be divided between three daughters listed in the will. However, at the time of settlement, Martha Beall and Eleanor Childs are both deceased, and their children are listed as heirs. Ezekiel and Susannah had at least two children (and probably more):

a. Elizabeth Anne Gott, born c.1798, of whom more.

b. Edwin Gott, also found as Edmond Gott (which is believed to be incorrect). Married to Anne Wilson in Anne Arundel County, Maryland, daughter of John Wilson and Elizabeth Gordon of Fauquier County, Virginia. They had children, including:

(1) Edwin Ezekiel Gott, born c.1824, of whom more.

Elizabeth Anne Gott
1798-1872

This daughter of Ezekiel Gott (1761) and Susannah Jackson Soper, was born c.1798 in Anne Arundel County, and died April 16, 1872. Married John Fletcher Wilson, born August 14, 1794 in Fauquier County, Virginia, died November 19, 1881 at Portland Manor, Anne Arundel County, Maryland; son of John Wilson and Elizabeth Gordon. Children, born at Allendale Farm in Anne Arundel County:

1. John Ezekiel Wilson, born February 21, 1825, died June 9, 1909 at Wakefield, Virginia. Married there October 19, 1848 to Amanda Susan Duvall, born December 10, 1826 at Glendale, Prince George's County; and second to Bettie Washington. Children:

a. Elizabeth Duvall Wilson, born August 18, 1849 at Wakefield, Virginia, and died there September 3, 1905. Married November 20, 1866 at St. James Church in Lothian, Maryland to Samuel Edwin Egerton, born November 18, 1839 at Chaptico, Maryland, died August 17,

1895 at Baltimore, son of Charles Calvert Egerton and Rebecca Callis. Ten children, born at Baltimore:

(1) Samuel Edwin Egerton, born December 7, 1867, died July, 1868
(2) John Fletcher Egerton, born January 6, 1869, died February 25, 1925 at Manila, Phillipines. Married to Susan Yeatman.
(3) Stuart Egerton, born November 21, 1870, died July 25, 1943. Married to Martha White.
(4) Samuel Edwin Egerton, born August 6, 1872, married April 7, 1896 to Bessie Appleton Tyler.
(5) Kennon Whiting Egerton, born April 4, 1874, died November 27, 1916. Married to Agnes Moore.
(6) Elizabeth Wilson Egerton, born April 25, 1876, died June 21, 1877
(7) Florence Beverly Egerton, born January 9, 1878 and died March 8, 1948 in Washington. Married March 27, 1901 to Walter Driscoll Smith.
(8) Martha Rankin Egerton, born January 9, 1880, died c.1967 at Washington. Married Ernest Joseph King.
(9) Helen Duvall Egerton, born Jnuay 14, 1881, died December 12, 1881.
(10) Ethel Wilson Egerton, born August 30, 1882, died November 26, 1884.

b. Mary Carr Wilson, born October 18, 1851 and died February 28, 1852.

2. Thomas Oswald Wilson, born September 16, 1820, died April 5, 1860.

3. Eliel Gott Wilson, born January 17, 1823, died August 15, 1828.

4. William Wesley Wilson, born June 10, 1827, died June 16, 1873. Married January 13, 1852 to Mary Calvert Egerton.

5. Eliel Soper Wilson, born May 13, 1829, died September 16, 1860.

6. Samuel Augustus Wilson, born October 12, 1832, died November 5, 1887. Married to Martha Wier.

7. Julius Edwin Wilson, born April 27, 1834 and died September 1, 1901. Married April 29, 1862 to Julia Carr.

8. Alvin Chesley Wilson, born May 17, 1836; married to Emily Compton.
9. Virgil Wilson, born c.1878; married Frances Carr.
10. Albert Wilson, born August 14, 1840, died July 1, 1893. Married October 4, 1883 to his double first cousin, Ella Gott, born September 21, 1861, died November 10, 1954 on Portland Manor, Anne Arundel, daughter of Edwin Ezekiel Gott (1824) and Sarah Tillard. They had children, listed under their mother's name, following.

Edwin Ezekiel Gott
1824-1901

This son of Edwin Gott and Anne Wilson was born c.1824 on Allendale Farm, Anne Arundel County, Maryland, and died c.1901. Married to Sarah Tillard, and had children, born on Allendale Farm in Anne Arundel County, Maryland:

1. Ella Gott, born September 21, 1861, died November 10, 1954 on Portland Manor, Anne Arundel, the estate of her husband. Married to her double first cousin, Albert Wilson, born August 14, 1840 on Portland Manor, died there July 1, 1893, son of John Fletcher Wilson (1794) and Elizabeth Ann Gott (1798). They had children, born at Portland Manor, Anne Arundel County:
   a. Elizabeth Gott Wilson, born July 23, 1884, died August 5, 1884
   b. John Fletcher Wilson, II, born August 8, 1885, died January 26, 1952. Married Emily Cummings Hammond.
   c. Sarah Eleanor Wilson, born November 16, 1886, died July 31, 1925. Married to John Sellman Woolen.
   d. Margaret Paret Wilson, born July 12, 1888, died c.1953 at Upper Marlboro. Married c.1923 to H. Guiger Clagett.
   e. Albert Wilson, Jr., married June 2, 1925 to Elizabeth Anne Parran.
   f. Elizabeth Augusta Wilson, born August 1, 1892, died October 22, 1918. Married June 4, 1918 to Hugh Fairchild Smith.
2. Edwin Gott, married to Elizabeth Hays.

3. William Gott.
4. Richard Gott.
5. Eleanor Gott, born c.1819.
6. Frances Gott, married to Eliel Wilson.

CHAPTER 6

Anthony Gott
1694-1781

This son of Richard Gott (1653) and his second wife Elizabeth Holland (1673) was born September 15, 1694 in Anne Arundel County, Maryland, and died c.1781, intestate. He was married to Jane, surname unknown. Anthony appeared in a number of records in Anne Arundel, as an agent, a merchant, a boat owner, and as the Constable of Herring Creek Hundred in 1737 and 1738. In 1752, he purchased the 162-acre tract known as *Daborne's Inheritance*, apparently his first land purchase. Anthony and Jane had children, born in Anne Arundel County:

1. Seaborn Gott, born December 10, 1736
2. Sybella Gott, died before 1766. Married to Henry Crandall, born August 4, 1735, died by 1758, son of Francis Crandall and Jane Atwood. Prerogative Court records of Anne Arundel County dated April 27, 1759 list Walter Gott and others as creditors of the estate of Henry Crandall; Joseph Gott and Nicholas Norman as next of kin; and Sibell (sic) Crandall as Administratrix. Same records dated October 15, 1761 list Sureties as Anthony Gott and Francis Crandall, with distribution to the unnamed widow of one third, and the residue to Henry Atwood Crandall, who is presumably a son. Administratrix was Isabell (sic) Crandall. Prerogative Court records dated June 16, 1767 relative to the estate of Sybella Crandall mention Henry Crandall, and the Administrator was Anthony Gott. Their child was:
   a. Henry Atwood Crandall.
3. Richard Gott, born c.1740, of whom more following.
4. Anthony Gott, Jr., died before 1800 in Calvert County, Maryland, where he had relocated c.1789, about the same time his brother Richard moved to Montgomery County. Married March 10, 1774 in Anne Arundel County to Ann Barker.
5. Joseph Gott, perhaps, born c.1739 (assume same age as his wife). He is found in several records of Anne Arundel County,

which suggest that he belongs in this family. He was married to Elizabeth Norman, born April 5, 1741, daughter of Nicholas Norman and Elizabeth Carr. Nicholas Norman left a will dated February 12, 1768, probated June 26, 1769, in which he named his children, including Elizabeth, wife of Joseph Gott. Nicholas Norman, Jr., born March 12, 1733 died intestate, without issue. Robert Franklin, Administrator of the estate, filed distribution on December 2, 1828, naming the heirs at law, including Elizabeth Gott, a sister of the deceased. As noted above, Joseph Gott and Nicholas Norman (probably Jr.) were listed as next of kin in the estate of Henry Crandall, who had married Sybella Gott, presumably the sister of Joseph Gott. On March 6, 1776, Joseph Gott and Ezekiel Gott, both of Herring Creek, were petitioners to form an independent militia company and both subsequently served in Captain Richard Weems' company. Joseph was deceased by August 10, 1802 when Robert Franklin made final distribution of his estate, giving sixths, although seven heirs were named, one of them being Elizabeth Gott, probably his wife. Children:

a.   Rachel Gott, married to Deale.
b.   Henrietta Gott, married to Deale.
c.   Mary Gott, married to Connor.
d.   Priscilla Gott, married to Richard Crandall before 1789.
e.   Elizabeth Gott, married to Franklin.
f.   Rispah Gott, born c.1769, died January, 1827.

Richard Gott
1740-1804

This son of Anthony Gott (1694) was born c.1740 in Anne Arundel County, and died c.1804 on his plantation, *The Fertile Plains*, in Montgomery County, having moved there about 1789 with his family. On December 15, 1788 Richard and his wife Eleanor sold *Daborne's Inheritance* to Nicholas Norman and Thomas Norman, in preparation for the move to Montgomery County. On May 10, 1792, Richard purchased from William Willcoxen the 396-acres tract called *The Fertile Plains*. The farm is located near present-day Boyds, and extended from the west bank of Little Seneca Creek to Buck Lodge Branch, both of which flow into Great Seneca Creek which empties into the Potomac River at Seneca, and remained in the family's possession for several generations thereafter. Richard was married to Eleanor Norris, born May 19, 1744 in Anne Arundel County, daughter of John and Mary Norris. Richard Gott left a will in Montgomery County, dated February 20, 1804, probated May 24, 1804, and recorded in liber E at folio 115; rerecorded in liber VMB 2, page 24, Register of Wills Office, Montgomery County. In his will, he names his wife Eleanor, and leaves the farm on which they lived to his son Richard Gott, who was named Executor. There were bequests of personal property and slaves to various children. He named three grandchildren: Elizabeth Harris, Thomas Harris and Nancy Harris; another son, and four daughters, as well as Sarah, his daughter-in-law, wife of his son Richard.

The will of Eleanor Gott was dated July 25, 1822, probated February 25, 1825 and recorded in liber O at folio 374, rerecorded in liber VMB 3 at page 310, in Montgomery County. She names a daughter-in-law Sarah Gott (apparently the wife of son Richard) and several other individuals, not all specified as to relationships. It appears that the children of Richard and Eleanor, all born in Anne Arundel County, included:

1. Jane Gott, born c.1765. Married there by license dated December 7, 1784 to Samuel Harris.
2. Mary Gott, born c.1767, died March 23, 1845 Parke County, Indiana. Married in Anne Arundel County by license dated November 29, 1785 to James Spencer.
3. John Gott, the eldest son, born c.1779, died July 8, 1833 in White County, Illinois. He may have remained in Anne Arundel County until his marriage there by license dated March 7, 1799 to Sarah Small Carter, daughter of Henry Carter and Rachel Small of Kent Island. John moved with his wife first to Kentucky, and on to Illinois. After his death, his widow was married second to Daniel G. Millspaugh of Illinois.
4. Richard Gott, born March 25, 1776, and of whom more.
5. Elizabeth Gott, born December 15, 1781, of whom more.
6. Eleanor Gott, died perhaps in Logan County, Kentucky. Married in Montgomery County by license dated September 12,

1801 to James Allnutt, son of Lawrence Allnutt and Eleanor Dawson.

7. Sybella Gott, died between 1846 and 1849, unmarried.

Richard Gott
1776-1858

This son of Richard Gott (1740), and his wife Eleanor Norris, was born March 25, 1776 in Anne Arundel County, and died December 12, 1858 at *The Fertile Plains* in Montgomery County, Maryland, near present-day Boyds, which he had inherited from his father. Scharff's *History of Western Maryland* states that Richard was a lieutenant during the War of 1812, which is apparently incorrect. He was a Lieutenant in Captain Robert T. Dade's company of Montgomery Militia, Third Regiment, but resigned his commission May 17, 1811, and did not serve in the War of 1812. He was married by license dated January 12, 1802 to Sarah Collinson of Anne Arundel County, daughter of Edward Collinson and Charity Waters of that county. Sarah was born May 20, 1784 in Anne Arundel County and died between August 1, 1826 and February 2, 1835. Eleven of their thirteen children grew to maturity. After the death of Sarah, he was married second by license dated February 2, 1835 to Cassandra Chew Smith, who had been previously married to McKinsey, and who also died before her husband, without children. Cassandra was born c.1783, appearing with Richard in the 1850 census of the Third District of Montgomery County. He was listed as a farmer, with $8,500 in real estate, and twenty-two slaves. Four of his children were then at home. Over time, Richard acquired several tracts of land, including part of *Beall's Goodwill*, part of *Mount Zion*, part of *It May Be Good In Time*, part of *Hempstone's Discovery*, part of *The Resurvey on Trouble For Nothing*, part of *Round Knoll*, part of *Mount Carmel*, and several other tracts. By the time of the 1831 tax assessment, his land holdings totalled 1,037 acres. Richard left a will dated February 22, 1856, probated December 22, 1858. It contains extensive listings of bequests of personal property, livestock, equipment, household furniture, slaves, and real estate, indicative of the wealth of Richard. The children of Richard included:

1. John Collinson Gott, born February 14, 1803, died October 19, 1871, single. In the 1850 census for the Third District, had living with him Leonard Plummer, born c.1805, listed as insane. Leonard was the son of John Plummer (1765) and an uncle of the two girls mentioned following, and John C. Gott was named his guardian. In the 1860 census for the Third District, he had Mary Plummer (1821) and Sarah A. Plummer (1825) living with him. Mary Plummer had $3,000 in real estate and $1,500 in personal property. John C. Gott had $500 in real estate and $5,150 in personal property. They are believed to be daughters of Joseph Plummer (1798) and Verlinda Veatch. In the Slave Census of 1867-1868, John C. was listed as owner of seven slaves, ranging in age from one year to forty-six. John and the two Plummer ladies were found next in the 1870 census of the Third District.

2. Mary Collinson Gott, born June 14, 1804, of whom more in Chapter 3.

3. Susan Ann Gott, born November 9, 1805, and of whom more as Child 3, following.

4. Richard Gott, Jr., born October 24, 1807, of whom more in Chapter 4.

5. Edward Collinson Gott, born March 5, 1809; died probably in Montgomery County, Missouri. Married at St. Peters Church in Poolesville by license dated May 18, 1832 to Rosetta Vauclin Bouic, born February 17, 1813 at Poolesville, in Montgomery County, daughter of Pierre Amable Tranquille Bouic (commonly found as Peter Bouic) and his wife, Darcus Veirs. Edward was married second November 17, 1859 to Mary E. Higgins, born c.1812. She was living in the household of Charles A. C. Higgins (1821) during the census of 1870 for the First District, with no other member of the family. She was living with the same family in the 1880 census of the Eighth District, and there designated as a sister of Charles A. C. Higgins. We did not find Edward Collinson Gott in any census record of Montgomery County.

6. Elizabeth Ann Gott, born May 16, 1810, died October 10, 1885, single. Buried at Monocacy Cemetery, Beallsville.

7. Eleanor Gott, born September 10, 1811, died c.1812

8. Jane Gott, born February 26, 1813, died August 18, 1821
9. Benjamin Collinson Gott, born May 28, 1814, and of whom more as Child 9, following.
10. William Collinson Gott, born February 10, 1816, died January 8, 1850, single.
11. Thomas Norris Gott, born April 1, 1818, of whom more as Child 11.
12. Sarah Eleanor Gott, born July 29, 1821, died September 22, 1843, single.
13. Nathan White Gott, born March 20, 1824, died single.

CHILD 3

Susan Ann Gott
1805-1882

This daughter of Richard Gott (1776) and Sarah Collinson was born November 9, 1805, died August 6, 1882 in Montgomery County, Missouri. Married in Montgomery County, Maryland by licesnse dated December 2, 1831 as his second wife to Samuel Benjamin White, born November 4, 1796 at Bucklodge, Montgomery County, Maryland, died December 3, 1878 in Missouri, son of Benjamin White (1752) and Rebecca O'Dell Chiswell. He had been married first March 23, 1820 in Montgomery County to Rebecca Darby, born c.1796, died March 9, 1821, daughter of Caleb Darby and Sarah Gartrell, leaving no children. Benjamin received from his father 100 acres of *Wolf's Cow* adjoining *Hanover*. Moved to Missouri, perhaps after the death of his first wife. Children, perhaps all born in Missouri:
1. Edward Collinson White, born November 4, 1832, died August 22, 1900 in Missouri. Married January 21, 1858 to Mary Catherine Crane, born in Mineola, Missouri and died there; daughter of George Washington Crane and Nancy G. Gresham. Children, perhaps born in Missouri:
   a. George White, married Mayme Smith.
   b. Charles William White, married Anna Della Scott and had children:
      (1) Lola White.

(2) Dora White.
c. Richard Collinson White, married Coreene Gregory and had children:
(1) William Clyde White.
(2) Dougal White.
d. Susan Ann White, married Dougal Baker, son of Clay Baker and Virginia Stevens.
e. Edward Collinson White, Jr., died in Mineola, Missouri. Married Mary Catherine Buck; children:
(1) George William White, born July 19, 1895, died December 23, 1966. Married to Nellie Hendrick.
(2) Marjorie White; married Ben Gregory.
2. William Henry White, born August 17, 1834, died December 18, 1918. Married April 17, 1860 to Catherine Minerva Covington and had children:
a. Benjamin M. White.
b. Sarah Ellen White.
c. Mary Virginia White.
3. Richard Gott White, born October 27, 1836, died April 22, 1917 in Missouri. Married twice, to sisters. First on February 21, 1867 to Anna M. Pegram, who died October 8, 1867. Married second August 15, 1877 to Mary Ella Pegram, born August 15, 1861, died January 5, 1920. Two children:
a. Mildred Susan White, born June 21, 1878; married June 21, 1898 to Rolla Samuel Paul. Children:
(1) Paulina Paul, born April 30, 1899
(2) Richard Samuel Paul, born December 16, 1903
(3) Mildred Paul, bon December 9, 1905
(4) Dorothy Elizabeth Paul, born March 1, 1919
b. Benjamin Edward White, born January 7, 1880 in Montgomery County, Missouri, died there February 7, 1885.
4. Benjamin White, born March 16, 1839, died June 10, 1926 in Missouri. Married January 21, 1868 to Julia Victoria Gregory, born 1851, died October 16, 1888. They had children, perhaps born in Missouri:
a. Margaret Rebecca White, born May 25, 1871, died February 25, 1920. Married February 14, 1905 to Jacob Rodgers. No children.

b. Susan Ann White, born February 4, 1873, died 1957. Married to Booker Jefferson Diamond.

c. Mary Elizabeth White, born 1875, single.

d. Benjamin Lee White, born October 31, 1877, died September 9, 1908

e. Roy White, born September 12, 1879, died January 5, 1972. Married March 27, 1907 Emily Ford, daughter of Labourn K. Ford and Emily Margaret Smith.

f. Richard Franklin White; married Sophia Barth.

g. Mabel Estella White, born March 20, 1882. Married to Alexander A. Clare.

h. John Grover White, born September 13, 1886, died October, 1982. Married to Louise Alice Kirn, the daughter of Andrew and Louise Kirn.

5. Susan Rebecca White, born September 4, 1841, died February 11, 1923 in Montgomery County, Missouri. Married March 20, 1860 to D. Franklin Graham, born July 16, 1826, died February 27, 1900; son of Robert Graham and Isabelle Galbreath. Children:

a. Mary Flora Graham, born 1860. Married Doctor Joseph Luther Jones. No children.

b. Susan White Graham, born 1861, died 1923. Married c.1880 to Robert Adams Baker.

c. Benjamin Richard Graham, born November 24, 1868, died November 20, 1940. Married November 24, 1890 to Emma Baker, the daughter of Sylvester Baker and Frances Stevens. One child:

(1) Frances Graham, born September 17, 1892.

6. Mary Ann White, born February 25, 1843, died at Mineola, Missouri. Married February 25, 1864 to George Washington Gregory, born 1834, died 1924. Children:

a. Anna Pegram Gregory, born November 10, 1866, died 1960. Married to William C. Crane.

b. Mary Ellen Gregory, born November 11, 1872, died 1960, single.

c. Benjamin Lee Gregory, born September 4, 1878; moved to California.

d. John Stanley Gregory, born September 29, 1879. Married to Gladys Wildman.
e. Georgia Gregory. Married to Arthur Allen, as his second wife.
f. Susan Elizabeth Gregory, died 1965.
g. Cecile Gregory; married Melvin Scott.
7. Sarah Ellen White, born February 22, 1845, died February 19, 1929 at Mineola, Missouri. Married February 22, 1868 to Reason Fletcher Windsor, and had children:
a. Mary Susan Windsor.
b. John Fleet Windsor.
c. Edward William Windsor.
d. Benjamin Windsor.

CHILD 9

Benjamin Collinson Gott
1814-1885

This son of Richard Gott (1776) and his first wife Sarah Collinson, was born May 28, 1814 on his father's farm, *The Fertile Plains*, near Boyds, in Montgomery County, Maryland, lived there throughout his life, and died April 23, 1885, intestate; buried at Monocacy Cemetery, Beallsville. He inherited the home farm of seven hundred acres, with the stone house his father built about 1812, which he improved and enlarged, adding another one hundred and fifty acres to the property. He was married twice, first by a license dated December 17, 1849 to Susan Ellen Darby, born April 15, 1831 at Dawsonville, died May 28, 1855 on the home farm, daughter of George Darby and Verlinda Allnutt, and had three children. Married second May 18, 1858 to Mariel Rebecca Cissel, born May 17, 1837 near Poolesville, died March 15, 1927, buried at Monocacy with her husband; the daughter of William Cissel (1803) and Rachel Sarah Williams (1812). Ten children were born to the second marriage. In 1864, Benjamin was elected a county commissioner, a post he did not seek, nor necessarily desire. Benjamin appeared with his second wife, Mary R., in the 1860 census of the Third District. Living with them were three children, apparently from his first marriage. Also in the household was Elizabeth A. Gott, born c.1810, with $4,500 in personal property. She was apparently his sister Elizabeth Ann, although the years of birth are somewhat different in the two census reports, although not unusual. Benjamin then owned $11,000 in real estate and $12,500 in personal property, rather substantial for the period. Benajmin was listed in the Slave Census of 1867-1868 as owner of thirteen slaves, the eldest being Vachel Duffin, born c.1809. Benjamin was next found in the 1870 census of the Third District (although when we transcribed the census, we apparently misread his age as 36 years, rather than 56 years). His second wife Mariel was there, and there were four children. Sister Elizabeth Ann was still living with them. Benjamin's wealth was steadily increasing; he then owned $20,580 in real estate and $6,759 in personal property. The 1880 census of the Medley District reports the family, headed by Benjamin and Mary, with six children at home. The children were born in Montgomery County, Maryland:

1. Sarah Verlinda Gott, born September 16, 1850, died February 4, 1851.
2. George Richard Gott, born February 10, 1852, died before December, 1903, an attorney in Baltimore. Married in Montgomery County November 27, 1878 to Mary Robertson Brewer, born 1853 to 1857, daughter of Doctor Nicholas Chiswell Brewer (1818) and his second wife Ruth Ellen W. Jones (1838). After the death of George Richard, Mary was married second December 5, 1903 to Harry W. Hunter.
3. Mary Amo Gott, born February 9, 1855, died April 4, 1892 in Prince George's County. Married by Montgomery County license dated January 31, 1879 to Dr. Stephen Beard of Prince George's County, born November 2, 1850, died April 5, 1893, son of Stephen Beard and Mary Susanna Collinson.
4. William Thomas Gott, the first child of the second family, born May 5, 1859, died September 19, 1875.
5. James Perry Gott, born February 17, 1861, died February 11, 1937; buried at Monocacy Cemetery, Beallsville, with other family members. Married October 27, 1886 to Annie Laurie Covington of Elkton, in Rockingham County, Virginia, born February 16, 1864, died November 30, 1896; buried with her

husband. James Perry Gott was married second January 30, 1902 at Frederick, Maryland to Lillian Pearl Atwell, born December 25, 1876 at Lovettsville, in Loudoun County, Virginia, and died April 23, 1940 at Rockville, Maryland; buried with her husband. She was the daughter of Richard Mason Johnson Atwell and Carrie Virginia Young, and had first been married to Henry R. Bird. James Perry Gott was head of household in the 1900 census of the Eleventh District, a widower with four children. His sister Elizabeth B. is living with him, single. Also listed is Emma R. Gott, widowed, born c.1836, designated as mother. She was of an age to be Mariel, but we can not explain the difference in the names. She had been the mother of nine children, six of whom were then living. The children of James Perry Gott were:

a. Lucille Warren Gott, born August 2, 1887 at Buck Lodge and died October 12, 1968 in Baltimore. Married January 17, 1916 in Georgetown to Ernest Chiswell Allnutt, born January 21, 1884, died January 13, 1928 at Baltimore; buried at the Monocacy cemetery near Beallsville, Montgomery County, son of Edwin Ruthvin Allnutt (1854) and Hester Anna Chiswell (1858). Children:
    (1) Ernest Chiswell Allnutt, born February 15, 1918.
    (2) James Gott Allnutt, stillbirth October 20, 1920.
b. Lula Beall Gott, born June 25, 1889 in Dickerson. Married February 26, 1913 in Montgomery County, Maryland to Oliver Belt White, born September 22, 1889, baptized September 22, 1889 at St. Peter's Church in Poolesville. He was a son of Lawrence Allnutt White (1854) of *Inverness*, and Annie Oliver Belt (1853). Four children:
    (1) Annie Laurie White, born August 24, 1917
    (2) Edward Oliver White, born January 21, 1919
    (3) Elizabeth Beall White, born February 23, 1920
    (4) Dorothy White, born June 30, 1921
c. James P. Gott, born September, 1891
d. Dorothy Virginia Gott, born October 1, 1903, died January 14, 1968. Married as his first wife January 24, 1924 to Bernard Trundle Brosius, born February 23, 1893,

died February 2, 1955 in Howard County, Maryland; buried at St. Mary's Cemetery, Barnesville, Montgomery County; son of Charles Thomas Brosius (1847) and Laura Virginia Trundle (1841). Divorced after having a daughter.

6. Ella Lee Gott, born September 3, 1863, died September 2, 1865.

7. Benjamin Collinson Gott, born April 20, 1866, died September 12, 1946 at Annapolis, Maryland; buried at Monocacy Cemetery, Beallsville. Head of household in the 1900 census of the Eleventh District, living next door to his brother Nathan. Benjamin was married December 9, 1891 to Elizabeth L. Lyons, who died February 23, 1969; buried at Monocacy. They had been married nine years at the time of the 1900 census, and had two children:

    a. Eleanor M. Gott, born November, 1893
    b. Elizabeth L. Gott, born September, 1897

8. Nathan Ellwood Gott, born July 13, 1868, died October 11, 1917; buried at Monocacy Cemetery. Married by Montgomery County license dated April 2, 1897 to Chloe Annie Warfield, born September, 1873, died January 5, 1964; buried with her husband; the daughter of John Thomas Warfield (1835) and Rachel Virginia Dorsey (1845). Head of household in the 1900 census of the Eleventh District, they then had one child. There were at least two:

    a. Muriel Virginia Gott, born February 15, 1898. Married January 31, 1920 to Dowell Jennings Howard, the son of Henry Howard and Florence Jones. Children:
        (1) Dowell Jennings Howard, Jr.; April 2, 1924
        (2) Marianna Virginia Howard, born Winchester, Va.
    b. Louise Warfield Gott, born March 10, 1903. Married November 20, 1924 to William Asbury Bowman.

9. Elizabeth Beall Gott, born February 26, 1871, died November 21, 1970, single. Buried at Monocacy Cemetery.

10. Eugene Cissel Gott, born August 16, 1873, died February 26, 1941 in Washington. Married June 16, 1897 to Harriet Barnes Meding of Washington, who died there October 7, 1957.

11. Hugh Leroy Gott, born January 7, 1879, died January 10, 1952 in Washington. In the 1900 census of the Bethesda District, listed as a clerk in the hotel operated by John McDermott (1860). Married September 21, 1908 Mary Elizabeth Keiser, who died December 14, 1955 in Washington.

CHILD 11

Thomas Norris Gott
1818-1903

This son of Richard Gott (1776) and his first wife Sarah Collinson, was born April 1, 1818 in Montgomery County, died September 5, 1903; buried at Monocacy Cemetery, Beallsville. Head of household in the 1850 census of Montgomery County for the Third District, Thomas was a farmer, owning $4,000 in real estate. Married in Montgomery County, Maryland by license dated September 25, 1843 to Eleanor White Chiswell, born September 18, 1822, died January 17, 1897; the daughter of William Augustus Chiswell (1783) and Sarah Newton Fletchall (1787); buried with her husband. In the 1850 census, they had four children. Head of household in the 1860 census of the Third District, Thomas then had $16,000 in real estate and $13,500 in personal property; with eight children at home. During the Civil War, Thomas Norris Gott was arrested and jailed for a time in Washington, suspected of having aided the Confederacy (which he probably had). He and his wife were next found in the 1870 census of the Third District, with seven children at home. He then owned $21,900 in real estate and $4,000 in personal property. Thomas and Eleanor were next found in the 1880 census of Medley District, with five of the children still at home. In the 1900 census of the Third District, Thomas is listed as a widower, with William, Ann Mary and Eugenia at home. Also living with him was his granddaughter Elma G. Davis (1874) and his granddaughter Eleanor M. Chiswell (1881). The children were:
1. Richard Thomas Gott, born October 17, 1844, died November 26, 1908. He was a doctor, and is buried at Monocacy Cemetery, Beallsville, with other family members in his father's plot. He was married November 11, 1873 to Alice Poole, born

October 1, 1851, died January 12, 1913, daughter of Doctor Thomas W. Poole (1804) and Evelina W. Hyde (1822); buried at Monocacy Cemetery in the plot of her father. The couple appeared in the 1880 census of the Medley District, living in a double household with the family of Evelina Poole, born c.1822, a widow. Richard and Alice next appeared in the 1900 census for the Third District. It is there reported that they had been married for 28 years, and had no children. There was one unnamed child, stillbirth.

2. Sarah Ellen Gott, born June 29, 1846, died January 25, 1936. Buried at Monocacy Cemetery in her father's plot, with her husband. Married May 23, 1871 to Arundel Thomas Davis, born 1847, died February 8, 1937, the son of Joshua Davis (1803); buried at Monocacy. In the 1870 census for the Third District, Sarah E. was living with Ellen F. Mathews (1842), dealer in millinery and fancy goods. Sarah and Arundel Davis had children, including:

   a.   Thomas Harold Davis, buried August 24, 1872 at Monocacy with his parents; aged 3 years, 1 month, 5 days.

   b.   Elma G. Davis (or Eleanor), born c.1874, died November 19, 1958. Married to Clarence J. Coates.

3. William Chiswell Gott, born December 14, 1847, died July 31, 1937 at Gaithersburg. Buried at Monocacy Cemetery.

4. Ann Mary Gott, born March 28, 1850, died February 25, 1922; buried at Monocacy with her parents, single.

5. Elizabeth Susan Gott, born July 21, 1852, died December 3, 1926, buried in her father's plot at Monocacy, with her husband. Married October 25, 1876 to John Augustus Chiswell, III, born December 30, 1851, died June 7, 1924 at Licksville, son of John Augustus Chiswell, Jr. (1830) and Sarah Rebecca Phillips (1830). They had children, including at least:

   a.   Eleanor M. Chiswell, born c.1881.

   b.   Eugenia Gott Chiswell, born September 16, 1883, and died March 6, 1933; buried with her parents at Monocacy.

   c.   Mary Collinson Chiswell, born c.1886, died September 12, 1961, single.

d. Margaret White Chiswell, born December 7, 1887 (or January 11, 1879), died January 11, 1919; buried with her parents at Monocacy, single.
5. Eugenia Gott, born January 13, 1854, died December 18, 1934; buried with her parents at Monocacy, single.
6. Benjamin Nathan Gott, born October 29, 1856, died May 20, 1928 and buried in the family plot at Monocacy Cemetery. Married April 18, 1883 at St. Mary's Catholic Church in Barnesville to Anna Mary Scholl, born April 23, 1859, died May 20, 1935, daughter of Henry Scholl and Caroline R. Murphy; buried with her husband. We found them first in the 1900 census of the Third District, with six children. They had been married 17 years and had been the parents of eight children, only six of whom were still living. The children were:

    a. Caroline Eleanor Gott, born January 28, 1884, died October 15, 1970; buried at Monocacy. Married May 13, 1908 to Marion Templeman Beall, born April 30, 1877, died June 1, 1963; buried at Monocacy. Ten children.

    b. Benjamin Thomas Gott, born April 23, 1885, died April 15, 1942 in Montgomery County. Married December, 1908 to Myrtle Best, born March 29, 1891 in Virginia, died July 1, 1970. A daughter.

    c. Mary Eloise Gott, born February 4, 1887, died July 26, 1955, buried at Monocacy. Married October 3, 1906 Linwood J. Hays, and had six children. Mary Eloise was apparently married second to Millard, and is buried at Monocacy in the Benjamin J. Hays plot, who may be her son. Buried there also are: Thomas Preston Hays, born January 20, 1910, died November 25, 1981, CBM, US-Navy, WWII; and Mary E. (Hays) Hardy, born June 6, 1927, and died October 5, 1956; who may be two more children of Linwood and Mary Eloise.

    d. Mabel Claire Gott, born April 10, 1889, died December 31, 1941 in Silver Spring, Maryland. Married April 27, 1918 to Miller Aiken Cassedy, born October 8, 1887, died February 10, 1948 at Rockville. Two children.

    e. Richard Gott, stillbirth April 14, 1892

f. Richard Gott, second use of the name, born October 24, 1894, died March 29, 1965. Married April 10, 1921 to Estelle Fromeyer, born at Gettysburg, Pennsylvania. Five children.

g. Anna Dorothy Gott, born July 2, 1899, died September, 1899.

h. Virginia Clark Gott, born November 6, 1900. Married April 2, 1929 to John Fendall Coughlan and had four children.

i. Kathleen Frances Gott, born April 5, 1896, died December 26, 1981; buried at Monocacy. Married November 16, 1918 Thomas Leonard Hays, Jr. and had two children

7. Dora Isabella Gott, born April 20, 1860. Married April 15, 1890 to John Calhoun Carr, born in Leesburg, Virginia. They had at least one son, born at Leesburg:

a. Thomas Gott Carr, born May 17, 1892, died February 25, 1959 at Vienna, Virginia. Married December 26, 1917 in Washington to Margaret Ellen Beall, born March 20, 1898 at Leesburg, died August 3, 1972 Falls Church, Virginia, daughter of Harry C. Beall and Margaret T. Tavener. At least one son:

(1) Harry Gott Carr, born May 5, 1922 at Leesburg, died September 29, 1997 at Vienna, Virginia. Married in Washington August 20, 1947 to Anne Carroll Hansford, born October 24, 1927 at Washington, died December 7, 1995 at Vienna, Virginia. They had children:

(a) Harriet Anne Carr.

(b) Carroll Hansford Carr, married to David Lee Hiner, and second to James Carroll Clements.

(c) Thomas Henry Carr.

(d) Patricia Lynn Carr.

Elizabeth Gott
1781-1854

This daughter of Richard Gott (1740) and Eleanor Norris (1744) was born December 15, 1781, died June 28, 1854, probably in Virginia. Married in Montgomery County by license dated January 27, 1801 to Thomas Dawson Allnutt, born March 13, 1777, died February 12, 1837; all in Montgomery County, Maryland. He was a son of James Allnutt and Virlinda Hawkins Dawson. The library of the Montgomery County Historical Society contains several volumes of research relative to the Allnutt, Darby and Chiswell families of Montgomery County, and it is not our purpose to here repeat that extensive information. We will therefore simply record the first generation of this family, and refer the reader to those works for the more definitive genealogy. Children:

1. Richard Gott Allnutt, born September 6, 1802
2. Sebell Allnutt, born November 4, 1803
3. James L. Allnutt, born February 2, 1805
4. Thomas H. Allnutt, born April 8, 1808
5. Washington Allnutt, born May 15, 1810
6. John Hanson Allnutt, born November 13, 1813, died April 2, 1900. Married May 31, 1838 to Elizabeth Jane Jarboe, who died March 14, 1843. Married second June 21, 1863 to Anna E. Offutt, who died January 25, 1902. They had children:
   a. Mary Effie Allnutt, born March 5, 1865, of whom more.
   b. John Hanson Allnutt, Jr., born July 26, 1867, married August 22, 1895 to Betty M. Padgett.
   c. Ellen Grace Allnutt, born July 24, 1876
7. Eleanor L. Allnutt, born June 16, 1815
8. Robert G. Allnutt, born October 19, 1817
9. William N. Allnutt, born March 6, 1819

Mary Effie Allnutt
1865-1936

This daughter of John Hanson Allnutt (1813) and Anna E. Offutt was born March 5, 1865, and died January 22, 1936. Married March 4, 1884 to John William Poole, Jr., born February 5, 1858, died February 12, 1937, son of John William Poole and Mary Margaret Stiles. They appeared in the 1900 census for the Third District, having been married 16 years, and the parents of seven children, all still living, and at home. The children were:

1. Mamie Lee Poole, born November 29, 1884, died March 14, 1952. Married to Benjamin F. Poole, and had children:
    a. Earl Poole.
    b. Benjamin F. Poole, Jr.
    c. John D. Poole.
    d. Pauline Poole.
    e. Eugene Poole.
2. John Hanson Poole, born March 4, 1886, died July 21, 1909. Married to Mary A. Connel.
3. Anna Mary Poole, born July 26, 1889, married June 29, 1910 to Herbert N. Vinson, and had children:
    a. Eleanor Vinson.
    b. Herbert N. Vinson, Jr.
    c. Bernard Vinson.
4. Lelia Eleanor Poole, born October 2, 1892, died April 20, 1970. Married to Charles Mossburg and had at least two sons:
    a. Ross Mossburg.
    b. Frank Mossburg.
5. Raymond Jerome Poole, born March 31, 1895
6. Robert Allnutt Poole, born April 21, 1897, died November 10, 1951. Married to Blanche McGee.
7. Paul Raphael Poole, born May, 1900, married to Lucy Napier and had at least two children:
    a. James R. Poole.
    b. Francis Poole.
8. Howard Eugene Poole, married to Willie Benson Webster.
9. Joseph Hugh Poole, born March 4, 1907 at Poolesville, died April 15, 1953 at Potomac, Maryland. Married March 4, 1933 to Elsie Mae Windsor, born April 22, 1913 at Potomac, died July 28, 1989 in Washington, D. C., the daughter of Joseph Edward Windsor (1880) and Geneva Gray (1885). A son:
    a. Joseph Hugh Poole, Jr., married to Anna Barbara Tripp and had a daughter:
        (1) Joanna Lee Poole, married to Brian Lee Martin.

CHAPTER 7

Mary Collinson Gott
1804-1890

This daughter of Richard Gott (1776) and Sarah Collinson (1784) was born June 14, 1804 at Bucklodge, died October 4, 1890, buried at Monocacy Cemetery at Beallsville. Married in Montgomery County by license dated December 14, 1824 to Joseph Chiswell White, born August 15, 1798 in Montgomery County, Maryland, and died December 6, 1886; buried Monocacy Cemetery near Beallsville; son of Benjamin White (1752) and Rebecca O'Dell Chiswell. It should be noted that on page 96 of the book, *Monocacy Cemetery, Beallsville, Montgomery County, Maryland,* by Elizabeth R. Frain, 1997, lists this individual as Joseph Collison White, apparently in error, transcribing his wife's middle name to his. (Absent that one error that I have detected, the book is a great addition to the genealogical resources of the county). It is said that at one time, Joseph owned the largest number of slaves in Montgomery County. According to one record found, an inventory taken in 1865 when slaves were freed noted that he then owned thirty-two. The 1850 census reports nineteen. His family is also there reported, at which time there were four children at home. They appear again in the 1860 census, with two children still at home. Also living with them at that time is Sarah Taneyhill, born c.1834, but not identified as to relationship. In 1860, Joseph had real estate valued at $12,750 and $15,100 in personal property, sizable holdings for that period. His will is filed in liber RCW 15 at folio 97 in Montgomery County records. Joseph received under his father's will "all of my plantation where I now live, except the tanyard, being parts of *Liberty, Albany* and *Wolf's Cow,* which apparently contained about 85 acres. He expanded his holdings to 440 acres of those two tracts, plus part of *Albany.* The couple appear again in the 1870 census for the Third District, with real estate now valued at $15,000 and one child still at home. At his death, Joseph left his farm to his son, John Collinson White (1833), with the provision that John pass the farm to his sons (not his wife), so that the property would remain in

White ownership. Pages from the family Bible were found in the White family file at the library of the Montgomery County Historical Society. Certain of the dates given following are taken from the Bible, and in some cases differ slightly from those found in other sources. We tend to accept the Bible dates. It is said that the home farm was known as *Mount Carmel*, formerly being *Gott's Mill*, and that General Stonewall Jackson once dined there with the family. Children:

1. Richard Gott White, born October 22, 1826 at Bucklodge, Maryland, died January 3, 1879; buried at Monocacy cemetery. His death was from blood poisoning, resulting from his having been thrown from a horse. Married January 4, 1853 to Huldah Ann Piles, born August 28, 1830, died December 19, 1910 at Barnesville; buried at Monocacy with her husband. She was a daughter of Hilleary Piles (1803) and Matilda Brewer (1806); both buried at Monocacy cemetery. Richard was a contractor, building part of the Baltimore and Ohio rail lines, stores and bridges. He was primarily a farmer, but also served as County Commissioner. They appear in the 1870 census for the Third District of Montgomery County, where he is listed as a carpenter, with real estate valued at $14,000 and $2,583 in personal property, comparatively well-to-do for the period; with one child. Also living with them are two farm laborers, both black; Winfield S. Johnson, born c.1854, and Charles Scott, born c.1856. Richard and Huldah had children:

   a. Albert White, born November 18, 1855, died August 4, 1858; buried at Monocacy cemetery.

   b. Hilleary Herndon White, born November 18, 1859, died July 1, 1862; buried at Monocacy.

   c. Thomas Oliver White, born August 20, 1862, died December 15, 1934; buried at Monocacy. Living with his parents in 1870. He attended Emerson Institute in Washington, D. C. and then took charge of his father's farm of about 550 acres; later purchasing another farm of about the same size. Married December 5, 1883 at Barnesville, Montgomery County, Maryland, to Annie Estelle Pyles, born November 25, 1861, died February 7, 1926; buried with her husband; daughter of Richard Thomas Pyles and

Laura V. Hawkins. Their marriage was the first one held in Christ Church at Barnesville. At least two daughters:

(1) Laura Virginia White, born January 2, 1886 at Barnesville and died May 21, 1968 at Alhambra, California. Buried at the Monocacy cemetery near Beallsville, Maryland.

(2) Mary W. White, married June 10, 1913 to William J. Lankford, of Laurel, Maryland. Two children.

   d.   Herndon White, died August 13, 1879; buried Monocacy.

2. Susan Ann White, born December 23, 1828 at Bucklodge, died December 27, 1895 in Kentucky. Married January 8, 1850 in Montgomery County, Maryland to Alexander Dade, born November 20, 1825, died 1908 in Kentucky, the son of Robert Townsend Dade (1787) and Ruth Simmons (1790). At the time of the 1850 census, Alexander and Susan were living in the home of his parents, having been married that year. They had a large family, born either in Montgomery County, Maryland, or in Kentucky. They appeared in the 1860 census for the Third District of Montgomery County, Maryland, with six children, born in Maryland. At the time, Alexander was listed as a farmer, with $4,000 in real estate and $6,800 in personal property. He was a slave owner, found in the Slave Index of Montgomery County for 1867-1868 with four slaves: Henry Offutt, born c.1840; James Beall, born c.1847; Eliza Beall, born c.1844; and William Beall, born c.1861. In the 1870 census for the Third District, Alexander is listed as a farmer with $6,300 in real estate and $1,750 in personal property. There are seven children at home, all born in Maryland; a number of them are buried at Monocacy Cemetery, Beallsville, in the Joseph C. White plot. The children were:

a.   Joseph Townsend Dade, born March 13, 1852. Married March 9, 1875 to his first cousin, Susan Ruth Dade.

b.   Richard Gott Dade, born January 9, 1853

c.   Mary Ruth Dade, born April 25, 1855, died September 11, 1863

d.   Ernest Dade, born December 19, 1856 in Kentucky.

e.   Melvin Dade, born c.1858, died March 16, 1880. He was also found as Melville in one of the census returns.

f. Serena Elizabeth Dade, born January 22, 1860, died February 4, 1863

g. Wade Hampton Dade, born September 10, 1861, died February 12, 1863.

h. Thomas Collinson Dade, born February 21, 1863, died October 27, 1863

i. Robert E. L. Dade, born c.1865

j. Alexander Dade, born c.1867

k. Sallie W. Dade, born c.1868

l. John S. Dade, born c.1869

m. Alonzo Dade, born February 10, 1871, died June 30, 1871

3. Thomas Henry White, born September 20, 1831 at Bucklodge, Montgomery County, Maryland; died January 19, 1930 at Glen Olden, Pennsylvania; buried at Monocacy. He served as a private in the 35th Virginia Cavalry, Army of the Confederacy. He reportedly served under Colonel E. V. White of Leesburg, and for a time was scout and courier for General Robert E. Lee. Captured at Beverly Ford during the battle of Brandy Station, June 9, 1863, and imprisoned at Old Capitol Prison in Washington, D. C. until exchanged June 25, 1863 at City Point, Virginia. Married December 18, 1855 in Montgomery County, Maryland to Mary Ellen Gott, born October 14, 1834, died May 26, 1890. He was married second January 29, 1895 to Laura Richard Gott, born August 11, 1850, and died February 22, 1926; buried at Monocacy. The two girls were sisters, daughters of Richard Gott, Jr. and Mary Elizabeth Trundle. Thomas appears as head of household in the 1860 census for the Third District of Montgomery County, with his first wife, Mary E., and three of their children. Also living with them was Solomon Grimes, born c.1851, not otherwise identified. The family appears next in the 1870 census with the four children then living. Nine children were born to the first marriage, and one child was born to the second marriage:

a. Richard White, born September 5, 1856 at Poolesville, Montgomery County, Maryland, died April 10, 1927 at Chico, California. Married January 22, 1892 to Flora Earll, or Florence Easell.

b. Henry White, born February 25, 1858, died March 23, 1862; buried at Monocacy cemetery.

c. Willis White, born September 26, 1859, died August 2, 1863; buried at Monocacy.

d. Mary Estelle White, born December 18, 1861, died February 27, 1963; buried at Monocacy. Married March 21, 1887 in Montgomery County to William Franklin Elgin and lived in Glen Olden, Pennsylvania, where her father died at her home. Doctor William Franklin Elgin was born September 16, 1861 at Poolesville, died April 18, 1938; buried at Monocacy with his wife; son of James Burton Elgin and Sarah Taylor. Dr. Elgin was a yellow fever expert, associated with Dr. Walter Reed in that research. At least two daughters are also buried there:

(1) Mary Ellen Elgin (also reported as Mary White Elgin), born December 9, 1889, died February 16, 1987. Married to Herbert Dixon Senat, born February 17, 1886 at Norwood, Pennsylvania, and had three children. Two more later marriages.

(2) Franklyn Estelle Elgin, born July 3, 1899, and died March 1, 1968 at Delaware, Pennsylvania; apparently single.

e. Joseph Thomas White, born September 24, 1865 in Poolesville, died October 14, 1933; buried at Monocacy. Married November 25, 1889 at Poolesville, Maryland, to Sarah Estella Brunner, born November 27, 1868, died January 5, 1929 at Washington Grove, Maryland, the daughter of William L. Brunner, and Julia Margaret Miller; buried at Monocacy with her husband. Children:

(1) William Rodney White, born 1890, of whom more

(2) Amy R. White, born December 17, 1893, died February 15, 1971, single.

(3) Thomas Earl White, married to Addie Archer and had two daughters.

(4) Alvin E. White, born 1896, died February, 1898

f. Alvin Hampton White, born October 1, 1867 at Poolesville, died February 8, 1929 in Pennsylvania and married to Elizabeth Simpson.

g. Edgar Gott White, born February 8, 1871 in Poolesville, died 1960, single.

h. Maurice White, born June 20, 1875, died July 31, 1876; buried at Monocacy cemetery.

i. Oliver Collinson White, born May 14, 1878, died June 22, 1880; buried at Monocacy.

j. Thomas Henry White, Jr., born November 22, 1895; died that day, and buried at Monocacy cemetery.

4. John Collinson White, born December 3, 1833 at Bucklodge, died August 28, 1910; buried at Monocacy. He was a Civil War veteran, with a Confederate marker at his grave. Married September 7, 1865 to Ann Ellen Grace Boteler, born April 24, 1841, died March 20, 1917; buried at Monocacy; daughter of Henry Boteler of Edward and Martha Priscilla Boteler. They are found in the 1870 census for the Third District, living next door to his parents, with her name listed simply as Grace. There were then three children in the family. Children, all buried at the Monocacy cemetery with other family members:

a. Edward C. White, born c.1868, died April 8, 1878. This is a cemetery record, although the 1870 census clearly shows a child named John C., born c.1867, who is apparently this same individual, named for his father.

b. Mary Priscilla White, born May 21, 1868, died May 22, 1945. Married January 11, 1893 in Montgomery county to Henry Elias Perry Soper, born November 8, 1868, died September 4, 1949 and buried at Monocacy; son of Elias Perry Soper. They had children, born at Bucklodge:

(1) Edna Grace Soper, born August 24, 1895, died December 28, 1967; buried in Herndon, Virginia. Married March 22, 1919 to Charles Thomas Reed, born at Herndon, August 30, 1899, died February 14, 1948 at Dawsonville, Maryland; buried at Herndon with his wife. Seven children:

(a) Mary Virginia Reed, died young.

(b) Franklin Eugene Reed.

(c) Edith Augusta Reed, a twin.

(d) Annette Louise Reed, a twin.

(e) Betty Frances Reed.

      (f)   Charlotte White Reed.

      (g) William Thomas Reed.

  (2) Leona White Soper, born November 29, 1897, died April 26, 1983.

  (3) Lingan Dow Soper, born January 24, 1900, and died July 15, 1980; buried in the Monocacy Cemetery. His wife was Alice Louise Haller, born June 1, 1903 and died April 2, 1969; also buried at Monocacy.

  (4) Daisy Collinson Soper, born September 2, 1901.

  (5) Paul Mackley Soper, born May 25, 1906, died May 14, 1907

  (6) Alice Boteler Soper, born April 14, 1911, and died January 19, 1978.

c. Henry Boteler White, born March 31, 1870 at Bucklodge, died July 28, 1950. Married December 21, 1897 to Sarah Elizabeth Bowman, born November 17, 1873, died February 5, 1960; buried at Monocacy cemetery near Beallsville with her husband; daughter of William Harrison Bowman and Catherine Elizabeth Darby. In the family folder at the library of the Montgomery County Historical Society, there is a letter from his children to the Maryland-National Capital Park and Planning Commission, dated June 20, 1970, requesting official recognition of White's Store Road, in honor of their father. The letter states that from about 1936 to 1950, Henry operated White's Store at the intersection of the Dawsonville-Bucklodge Road and White's Store Road. It was signed by his children, with their dates of birth:

  (1) Edith Blanche White, born April 8, 1899 At Buck Lodge, died August 29, 1984 at Homewood Retirement Center, Frederick; buried at Monocacy, single.

  (2) Raymond Elwood White, born August 25, 1903. (Name also reported as Raynard Elwood). Married November, 1924 to Helen Virginia Whipp, born January 25, 1906, died June 25, 1943 and buried at Monocacy cemetery. After her death he married second June 9, 1945 to Helen Esther St. Claire, born

September 19, 1907 in Baltimore. Four children from his first marriage and one from the second:
    (a) Raymond Elwood White, Jr.
    (b) John Joseph White.
    (c) Robert Boteler White, born March 17, 1939.
    (d) Wilford Lee White, born July 19, 1940
    (e) Helene Elaine White, born October 9, 1946
(3) Helen Catherine White, born July 20, 1904, died September 25, 1906
(4) Grace Elizabeth White, born October 3, 1905, died April 5, 1995; buried at Monocacy. Married April 3, 1926 to Newton Gilbert Roberson, born October 23, 1904, died January 10, 1972; buried at Monocacy. They are likely the parents of, at least:
    (a) Mary Elizabeth Roberson, married to Luther Eugene Johnson, born May 5, 1926 and died March 18, 1997. He is buried in the same plot with Newton Gilbert Roberson and his wife, with Mary Elizabeth's name on the stone.
    (b) Edith Joyce Roberson.
(5) Nellie Boteler White, born December 8, 1907, died November 3, 1975. Married to Charles Garrett Cooley, Sr., a veterinarian, born April 5, 1904, died August 17, 1979. Two children:
    (a) Charles Garrett Cooley, Jr.
    (b) Lawrence White Cooley.
(6) Kathleen Dorothy White, born February 1, 1910, died 1987. Married December 24, 1927 to Edgar Ray Luhn of Rockville, born October 29, 1903 at Comus, Maryland. Three children:
    (a) Edgar Ray Luhn, Jr.
    (b) Dorothy White Luhn.
    (c) Donald Delano Luhn.
d. William Lingin White, born January 13, 1872, died May 19, 1939 at Gaithersburg; buried Monocacy cemetery near Beallsville. Married January 28, 1903 in Rockville to Mary Virginia Bowman, born 1876, died December 29, 1943 at Barnesville; buried with her husband,

daughter of William Harrison Bowman and Catherine Elizabeth Darby. Children:

(1) Mary Eleanor White, born July 25, 1904, died October 26, 1970; buried in same plot with William Lingin White at Monocacy. Married July 7, 1928 to Robert Lamont Thurston, born July 7, 1904, died March 19, 1986 and buried there also.

(2) William Marshall White, born October 20, 1908, died April 4, 1991, buried at Monocacy cemetery near Beallsville. Married August 23, 1930 to Margaret Eleanor Linthicum, born December 11, 1908 at Hyattstown, Maryland, died February 8, 1993 and buried with her husband. Three children:
   (a) Maryanne White, married to Warne.
   (b) Barbara Jane White, married to Belecanech.
   (c) John Collinson White.

(3) Catherine Bowman White, born July 7, 1910, died July 2, 1989. Married August 26, 1933 to William Pierce Hunter, Jr., born August 11, 1911, died November 5, 1970; buried at Monocacy cemetery.

(4) Estelle Elizabeth White, born July 9, 1914. Married first 1939 to Harold Benjamin Brooks, born May 14, 1912, died October 22, 1970; buried at Monocacy; one child. Married second 1955 to Einar Charles Norman, and had two children.

(5) William Lingin White, Jr., born November 10, 1916, died November 7, 1983; buried at Monocacy cemetery. Married 1937 to Margaret Lucille Bean, and had twelve children. There is a *Sentinel* newspaper notice dated May 10, 1937 which states that William L. White, Jr., son of Mr. and Mrs. William L. White, Sr., of Gaithersburg, was married May 1, 1937 to Evelyn Bean in Washington. The names and the time frame are correct; we can not explain the discrepancy in information. Children:
   (a) Charles David White.
   (b) Richard Eugene White.
   (c) Robert William White.

(d) E. Marie White.

(e) Mary Virginia White.

(f) William Granville White.

(g) Suzanne White.

(h) Gertrude Jeanette White.

(i) Gerald LeRoy White.

(j) Infant White, stillbirth.

(k) Infant death, June 6, 1939

(l) Infant death, girl, December 7, 1953

e. Joseph Collinson White, born January 21, 1874, died September 9, 1947; buried at Monocacy cemetery near Beallsville. Married February 8, 1905 Washington, D. C. to Mary Lucile Jones, born December 27, 1880, died May 30, 1964; buried with her husband.

f. Charles Ernest White, born February 14, 1876 at Bucklodge, Maryland, died October 24, 1944 in Boyds; buried in Monocacy cemetery near Beallsville with his wife. Married January 15, 1908 to Abbie May Specht, born 1874, died March 17, 1964. His obituary in the *Frederick Post* of October 25, 1944 furnishes information as to some of his siblings, and his children, with their residence as of 1944. In addition, *Monocacy Cemetery, Beallsville, Montgomery County, Maryland,* by Elizabeth R. Frain, 1997, Willow Bend Books, Lovettsville, Virginia, provides information about the family. It is an invaluable resource when searching many branches of the White family, and their collateral lineages, highly recommended for the library of any genealogist searching upper Montgomery County families. The children were:

(1) John Collinson White, born 1908, died May 23, 1937; buried at Monocacy.

(2) Michael Specht White, of Boyds, born December 3, 1909.

(3) Charles Ernest White, Jr., born February 19, 1913, died October 31, 1991. Married to Maxine E. Ruffner, born December 24, 1916, died February 24, 1972. Buried at Monocacy cemetery. Two children:

(a) Carol Sue White, married Eugene Hurd, born 1938 in Virginia, died June 3, 1990; buried at Monocacy. Two children.

(b) Shirley White, married Charles Lester Poole, born April 29, 1930. Two children.

(4) Donald Coplan White, of Dickerson, born September 25, 1915, died November 19, 1994; buried at the Monocacy cemetery. Married November 17, 1937 in Ellicott City, Maryland, to Gertrude H. Ganley, born in Boyds. A daughter:

(a) Anna Marie White, born February 26, 1939, married June 24, 1958 to David Garth Perry, born June 13, 1934, son of Harry Clay Perry (1896) and Nannia Frances Bentz (1906) of Gaithersburg, Maryland. Children:

1. Michele Denise Perry, born May 15, 1961. Married November 17, 1990 to Charles Dwayne Federline, born September 20, 1961. Children:

   a. Charles Kenneth Federline, born: August 12, 1993

   b. Lauren Marie Federline, born September 11, 1994

2. Nicole Marie Perry, born May 3, 1972

3. David Garth Perry, Jr., born December 4, 1974

(5) Betty Warnetta White, born August 2, 1911, died April 23, 1991. Married to Albert D. Reesch, of Washington, born September 29, 1900, died April 22, 1982. Both buried at Monocacy cemetery.

g. Susan Ann White, born May 23, 1878, died February 2, 1934. Married to James S. Moore, born February 7, 1864, died February 29, 1936. They are buried in their own family plot at Monocacy cemetery, Beallsville. In the same plot are three other individuals of an age to be their daughters, each of whom were married. Burial records have each of them with the maiden name Moore; they were children of this couple, with a fourth child as well:

(1) Mildred White Moore, born August 27, 1904, died March 22, 1942; married to James Leroy Harris.

(2) Helen Boteler Moore, born October 1, 1906, died September 26, 1941; married April 20, 1929 to Ward W. Oattington; married second to Marcel Zimmerman.

(3) Ethel Virginia Moore, born August 26, 1908, died September 14, 1962. Married first September 1, 1934 to Luther Roland King. Married second April 3, 1947 to John Holt Brown.

(4) Barbara Collinson Moore, born March 27, 1918, died October 24, 1984; married November 27, 1942 to Herman Henry Ladson, born November 5, 1916. Two children.

h. Sarah Elsby White, born July 10, 1880, died November 11, 1966. Married April 25, 1906 John Jacob Umstead, of Poolesville, born January 29, 1872, died March 17, 1941, the son of Richard S. Umstead and Frances Ella Austin. Both are buried at Monocacy cemetery, near Beallsville. Children:

(1) Frances Ellen Umstead, born November 11, 1907 at Boyds, Maryland, died May 10, 1995; buried at Monocacy cemetery near Beallsville. Married three times; first to Robert Thompson Dayhoff; second to William Linwood Sears; third to Paul Leonard Eader.

(2) Emma Grace Umstead, born March 31, 1912. Married June 1, 1933 to Douglas Edwin Horine, born November 21, 1911 in Pennsylvania. They had two children.

i. Elizabeth Virginia Sprecher White, born May 6, 1882 at Bucklodge, Montgomery County, Maryland, died November 2, 1977. Married February 8, 1905 John William Moore, born January 27, 1866, died April 1, 1954. Both are buried at Monocacy cemetery. He was a son of William Hempstone Moore and Barbara C. Boyer. Children:

(1) William Hempstone Moore, born January 26, 1906 at Barnesville, Maryland. Married Blanche Veronica Marie Mende.

(2) Joseph Collinson Moore, born April 6, 1910 at Bucklodge, Maryland, died April 15, 1993. Married December 7, 1943 to Edna Carolyn Donahoe, born June 30, 1919 in Pittsburgh.

(3) John William Moore, Jr., born July 16, 1919 at Bucklodge, died April 13, 1975 at Boyds; buried at Monocacy cemetery. Married August 6, 1949 to Kathleen Patricia Bowen, born December 16, 1919 at Alfretta, Georgia, and had two children.

5. Sarah Rebecca White, born August 22, 1838, died January 19, 1880 in Washington, D. C.; buried at Monocacy. Living at home in 1870; married November 13, 1878 to Doctor Stephen Olin Richey, born 1848, died October 8, 1919 in Washington, D. C.; buried with his wife at Monocacy.

William Rodney White
1890-1953

This son of Joseph Thomas White (1865) and Sarah Estella Brunner (1868) was born 1890, died September 6, 1953, and is buried at Monocacy cemetery near Beallsville with numerous other members of the White families. He was married to Mary Elizabeth Walker, born November 16, 1892, died September 5, 1978 at Westminster Nursing Home, buried at Forest Oak Cemetery in Gaithersburg; the daughter of Nathan Asbury Walker (1865) and Frances Willard Hughes (1866). Seven children:

1. Joseph Rodney White, born September 14, 1914; married first Violet Stinnett; one son. Married second Catherine I. Becraft, born October 10, 1913, and had three children. Married third Mariam M. Cramer, born September 8, 1926; no children. His children were:
   a. Joseph Rodney White, Jr., died 1980
   b. Joyce D. White, born May 28, 1944
   c. Karla Kay White, born August 21, 1946
   d. Joseph Michael White, born August 10, 1947

2. Dorothy Elizabeth White, born November 17, 1915; married Charles E. Welty, born December 14, 1904. A son:
   a. Douglas MacArthur Welty, born February 14, 1943
3. Charles LeRoy White, born August 13, 1917; died February 13, 1962, buried at Forest Oak Cemetery in Gaithersburg. He was a staff sergeant, Co. A, 115th Infantry in the second world war. Married to Kate H. Detrick, born October 4, 1925 and had a son:
   a. Charles Stephen White, born December 14, 1953, and married June 4, 1977 to Susan Diane Adams, born October 8, 1957; daughter of Jesse Adams (1928) and Ruth Diane Fulks (1933).
4. William Earl White, born August 18, 1920; married to Barbara L. Kirby, born February 6, 1923. Children:
   a. Cheryl Lynn White, born March 25, 1944
   b. Charlotte Marie White, born September 18, 1947
   c. Dana L. White, born April 20, 1959
5. Betty Lee White, born November 10, 1925; married first George E. Viers, born April 20, 1921, and had one daughter. Married second Robert Eugene Viers, born September 26, 1926, and had three children:
   a. Deborah Jene Viers, born November 23, 1949
   b. Vickie Lee Viers, born September 23, 1954
   c. Robert B. Viers, born October 26, 1955
   d. Nancy Jene Viers, born November 12, 1957
6. Alvin H. White, born 1927; died February 8, 1929 at Washington Grove; buried at Monocacy cemetery.
7. William Rodney White, Jr., born October 4, 1930 in Washington Grove, died September 5, 1987 at his home on Muncaster Road in Montgomery County, Maryland; buried at the Laytonsville cemetery. Sergeant with forty-one months of service during the Korean War, suffered severe injuries during that conflict, received the Purple Heart, and was a member of the "Chosin Few," a veteran's organization of the few surviving men of the battle of the Chosin Reservoir. Married to Margaret E. Swann, born December 24, 1935. Two children:
   a. Mary Margaret White, born April 3, 1956
   b. William Rodney White, III, born August 1, 1964

CHAPTER 8

Richard Gott, Jr.
1807-1853

This son of Richard Gott (1776) and Sarah Collinson (1784) was born October 24, 1807 in Montgomery County, Maryland, and died August 23, 1853. Married November 11, 1833 to Mary Elizabeth Trundle, born April 10, 1816, and died September 29, 1886; buried at Monocacy Cemetery, Beallsville, with her husband, daughter of John Lewis Trundle (1776) and Mary Veatch (1776). They were found in the 1850 census for the Third District, where he was listed as a farmer, born in Maryland, with $7,100 in real estate, and five slaves. They then had six children at home. In the 1860 census of the Third District, Barnesville Post Office, Mary is listed as head of household, apparently widowed, and there are now seven children. She was fairly prosperous for the period, listed with $18,000 in real estate and $9,750 in personal property. In the Slave Census of 1867-1868, Mary E. Gott was listed as owning ten slaves, seven of them with the surname Hall, headed by Fanny Hall, born c.1817. Mary was next found as head of household in the 1870 census for the Third District, with John and Laura still at home, and owned $9,690 in real estate and $1,198 in personal property. The 1880 census of the Medley District lists Mrs. Mary Gott, living alone, of the proper age, a mill owner. Children were:

1. Mary Ellen Gott, born October 14, 1834, died May 26, 1890. Married December 18, 1855 in Montgomery County, Maryland to Thomas Henry White, born September 20, 1831 at Bucklodge, Montgomery County, Maryland; died January 19, 1930 at Glen Olden, Pennsylvania; buried at Monocacy, son of Joseph Chiswell White (1798) and Mary Collinson Gott (1804). The children and descendants of Mary Ellen Gott and Thomas Henry White are discussed under their father's name in Chapter 3, which see.

2. Sarah Elizabeth Gott, born January 15, 1837, died March 23, 1893. Married December 8, 1857 as his first wife to Elijah Veirs White, born August 29, 1832 at *Stoney Castle*, died

January 11, 1907 in Loudoun County, Virginia; son of Stephen Newton White (1793) and Mary Elizabeth Veirs (1791). He was married second November 28, 1894 to Margaret Bitting Baines in Philadelphia at the home of her brother. He served as Colonel in Confederate forces, commanding the 35th Regiment, Virginia Cavalry, during the Civil War. His exploits are documented in Montgomery County Historical Society Volume 21, No. 4, found in the White family file in the library at Rockville. The *Montgomery County Sentinel* of May 24, 1907 published an account of his services, written by Magnus S. Thompson, who had been a member of the Battalion. It is also in the White family file, with several other papers relative to Colonel White; all recommended reading, and too lengthy to repeat here. In upper Montgomery County, beyond Poolesville, can be found White's Ferry, the last of its kind, carrying cars from Maryland to Virginia. Originally known as Conrad's Ferry, it takes its present name from Colonel Elijah White who moved from Poolesville to a farm in Loudoun County. After the war, he returned to Leesburg, and became the Sheriff of the county, as well as involvement as Church Elder and preacher; banker and business-man, with a fancy goods store at Leesburg, the ferry crossing and warehouses along the river. He lived for a number of years at *Montresor*, and moved into Leesburg about 1895, where he built a large frame home in the Queen Anne style at the corner of Cornwall and Wirt Streets. A photo of *Montresor* shows a very large frame dwelling of two full floors, with five bay windows above in the roof line. There are eight full windows across the front of the first and second floors, indicating the size of the house. He and Sarah Elizabeth Gott had children, born Loudoun County, Virginia:

a. Stephen Newton White, born October 3, 1858, died January 18, 1862.
b. Melvin White, born 1860, died March 12, 1862
c. Mary Elizabeth Gott White, born April 18, 1861, died 1871.
d. Elijah Brockenborough White, born 1862, died April 13, 1926 in Loudoun County, Virginia. Lived in Baltimore,

but returned to Loudoun County about 1902, with children from a first marriage. He was married first January 12, 1887 in Loudoun County to Rose Lee Pancoast, born there February 13, 1865, died July 24, 1893 in St. Louis, Missouri; having had two children. Elijah was married secondly December 13, 1926 to Lalah Harrison, born 1871, died April 15, 1945 at Leesburg, Virginia. His children from the first marriage were:

(1) Hazelle White, born February 3, 1888 at Leesburg, Virginia, and died February 5, 1920. Married to Joel Chandler Harris, born February 3, 1888, died January 25, 1920.

(2) Jane Elizabeth White, born 1893 at Leesburg, died June 12, 1970.

e. Benjamin Veirs White, born October 14, 1865 in Loudoun County, Virginia, died May 18, 1931; buried at Union Cemetery in Leesburg. Married 1892 to Lillian Carter Brosius, born 1870, died December 23, 1951; buried with her husband. He was a mill operator at Leesburg, and had children:

(1) Lillian Veirs White, born September 22, 1893 and married November 6, 1920 in Loudoun County to John Alexander Tebbs, born March 9, 1893, son of Richard Henry Tebbs.

(2) Benjamin Heath White, born May 18, 1896, died November 26, 1969. Married Dorothy Murray.

(3) Elijah Veirs White, born August 12, 1899, and died August 28, 1965. Married Mary Putman, born November 21, 1905, died March 8, 1976.

(4) Albert Stephen White, born 1902, died 1965.

f. Inez Gott White, born 1868 near Leesburg, Virginia. Married February 13, 1895 in Loudoun County to John D. Gold, born 1868 at Wilson, North Carolina. Children:

(1) Margaret B. Gold.

(2) Inez Gold.

(3) Elizabeth Gold, married to Swindell.

g. Richard Gott White, born 1870, died before 1880

h. Ida White, born June 30, 1871 near Leesburg, Virginia, died March 27, 1907; buried there in Union Cemetery. Married November 15, 1892 to Isaac Trimble Long, born May 16, 1866 in Page County, Virginia, died February 9, 1956 at Herndon, Virginia; buried with his wife. They had children:

(1) Isaac Trimble Long, Jr.

(2) Elijah White Long.

(3) Garland Long.

(4) Ada Long.

(5) Inez Long, born March 10, 1906, died November 10, 1968.

i. John Gott White, born 1872 in Loudoun County, Virginia, died there February 3, 1934; buried in Union Cemetery. Married November 24, 1898 to Mary Beale Barney of Fredericksburg, Virginia, daughter of Joshua N. Barney and Anne Seddon Dornin, and had children, all born in Leesburg, Virginia.

(1) Helen B. White.

(2) Anne White.

(3) Elijah Brockenborough White, II.

3. Susan Ann Gott, born January 16, 1840, died March 2, 1862; buried at Monocacy.

4. Jane Sybill Gott, born July 15, 1842. Married to Robert Dade.

5. Ann Virginia Gott, born March 28, 1845, died February 25, 1922; buried with her husband at Monocacy Cemetery. Married January 6, 1869 to Benjamin John Jones, born October 24, 1840, died May 7, 1909; son of Lloyd S. Jones (1808) and Teresa Ann Beall (1812). The couple appeared in the 1870 census for the Third District, with their first child, but were not found in later census records. Near the chapel at Monocacy Cemetery, Beallsville, stands a stone honoring Maryland soldiers who served the Confederacy during the Civil War. One of the names inscribed there is Benjamin J. Jones. He served as a private, Co. B, 35th Virginia Cavalry. Child was:

a. Mary Alta Jones, born October 14, 1869, died June 15, 1873; buried with her parents at Monocacy.

6. John Spinks Gott, born January 24, 1848, died August 17, 1923; buried at Monocacy Cemetery. Married January 31, 1874 to Florence Elizabeth Hayes, born c.1852, died September 27, 1921; buried with her husband. They were found in the 1880 census of the Medley District, with two children. They next appeared in the 1900 census for the Eleventh District, with three sons at home, and the notation that there had been four children born, with three still living. The three were:
   a. Richard Brook Gott, born c.1874, died May 18, 1961; buried at Monocacy Cemetery. Married Nellie McDonald, born c.1874, died June 2, 1944; buried with her husband.
   b. John Forest Gott, born c.1879; listed as a school teacher in the 1900 census.
   c. Samuel Roger Gott, born June 23, 1882, died May 28, 1919; buried at Monocacy Cemetery.
   d. M. Luella Gott, died September 21, 1888; buried at Monocacy, and apparently the missing fourth child.
7. Laura Richard Gott, born August 11, 1850. Married January 29, 1895 to Thomas Henry White, born September 20, 1831 at Bucklodge, Montgomery County, Maryland; died January 19, 1930 at Glen Olden, Pennsylvania; buried at Monocacy, widower of her eldest sister, Mary Ellen Gott, and father of nine children by that marriage (see above). Laura was mother of one child:
   a. Thomas Henry White, Jr., born November 22, 1895; died that day, and buried at Monocacy cemetery.

CHAPTER 9

Robert Gott
died 1695

This individual is found in several references in Anne Arundel County, Maryland, but has not been identified within the families studied thus far. He is apparently the same Robert Gott who was transported to Maryland in 1669 on the *Nightingale*, out of Hull, England, John Hobson, Master. In 1693, Robert purchased a tract of land containing 40 acres of *Barren Point* and 200 acres of *Pascall's Choice*, which adjoined *Ram Gott Swamp*, then owned by Richard Gott (1653), son of the immigrant Richard Gott, who died in 1661. Surely Robert was related to the others, but how?

Robert left a will in Anne Arundel County, dated January 12, 1695, probated February 18, 1695. He left to son Robert (apparently his only son), the plantation bought of James Pascall, conisting of Barren Point and Pascall's Choice (or Chance). He then provided that the property would pass to his five daughters should Robert died without issue. His wife was Alice, named as Executrix and residuary legatee and, after the death of her husband, married secondly to William Smith. The children were:

1. Robert Gott, Jr., who was apparently not of age at the time of his father's death, and for whom Thomas Walker acted as guardian in matters dealing with the estate. In 1720, Robert Gott, Jr. sold his inheritance to James McIntosh of Anne Arundel County.
2. Florence Gott, married to Thomas Walker.
3. Rebecca Gott, born c.1690, died before December, 1716. Married November 4, 1707 to Thomas Gatewood, Sr., born c.1687, died c.1748, son of John Gatewood of Essex County, Virginia. Children, apparently born in St. James Parish, Anne Arundel County, Maryland:
    a. Joseph Gatewood.
    b. Ambrose Gatewood.
    c. Robert Gatewood.
    d. John Gatewood.

e. Sarah Gatewood.
f. Rachel Gatewood.
g. Elizabeth Gatewood, married to Thomas Haile.
h. Amy Gatewood, married to Thomas St. John.
i. Mary Gatewood.
j. Thomas Gatewood, Jr., born February 7, 1710, married to Frances Dix and had children. He is apparently the Thomas Gatewood who left a will in Anne Arundel County, dated September 14, 1753, proven June 13, 1758 in which he names only two of his daughters, Mary and Sarah. His wife, not named, is joint Executor with Joseph Fowler. The children were:
    (1) John Gatewood, married in Anne Arundel County November 1, 1771 to Anne Roberts Lambeth.
    (2) Mary Gatewood.
    (3) Sarah Gatewood.
    (4) Thomas Gatewood.
4. Mary Gott.
5. Ann Gott.
6. Margaret Gott.

CHAPTER 10

Miscellaneous Gott Family Members

In the course of research, a number of references were found to individual members of the Gott family, mentioned here. All names in the left column bear the surname Gott, either by birth or by marriage.

Individual	Event
Hallie	Born 03/13/1910, died 08/29/1969, married as his second wife William Hughes Walker, born 08/27/1901, died 01/24/1962, son of Nathan Asbury Walker (1865). No children.
Mary E.	Md 02/15/1872 to Richard Thomas Spates.
Rebecca	Born 03/20/1905; md 01/27/1926 to Robert McKendree Williams, born 07/22/1904, died 09/16/1995, buried at Monocacy; son of William McKendree Williams (1875) and Sarah Griffith White (1880).

BIBLIOGRAPHY

Adams, Katharine Beall. *Maryland Heritage-A Family History.* Hillsboro, NC Privately printed 1983

Allnutt, Anne C. *Allnutt, Chiswell, Darby, Dawson, White.* Genealogy Database Printouts. 1996. Library of the Montgomery County Historical Society. Rockville, Maryland.

Barnes, Robert. *Maryland Marriages, 1634-1777.* Baltimore, Md. Genealogical Publishing Co. Fifth printing 1995.

_____. *Maryland Marriages, 1778-1800*

_____. *Marriages and Deaths From the Maryland Gazette 1727-1839.* Baltimore. Genealogical Publishing Co. 1973

Bowman, Tressie Nash. *Montgomery County Marriages, 1796-1850*

Burke, Sir Bernard, Ulster King of Arms. *The General Armory of England, Scotland, Ireland and Wales, Volumes 1, 2 & 3..* Bowie, Md. Heritage Books, Inc. 1878, Reprint 1996

Buxton, Allie May. *Family of Harry and Rosa Hurley.* Manuscript; Montgomery County Historical Society, Rockville, Maryland.

_____. *The Family of Isaac Moxley.* Damascus, Md. 1984

_____. *Nehemiah Moxley, His Clagettsville Sons and Their Descendants.* Chelsea, Michigan. BookCrafters. 1989

Carothers, Bettie Sterling. *1776 Census of Maryland.* Westminster, Md. Family Line Publications. 1992

Cook, Eleanor M. V. *Guide to the Records of Montgomery County, Maryland, Genealogical and Historical.* Westminster, Md. Family Line Publications. 1997

Crozier. *The General Armory*

Cutler, Dona L. *The Genealogical Companion to Rural Montgomery Cemeteries.* Bowie, Md. Heritage Books, Inc. 2000

Day, Jackson H. *James Day of Browningsville, and his descendants, A Maryland Family.* Columbia, Md, private, 1976.

Dern, John P. and Mary Fitzhugh Hitselberger. *Bridge in Time, The Complete 1850 Census of Frederick County, Maryland.* Redwood City, CA. Monocacy Book Company. 1978

Eader, Edith Oliver & Trudie Davis-Long. *The Jacob Engelbrecht Marriage Ledger of Frederick County, Maryland 1820-1890.* Monrovia, Md. Paw Prints, Inc. 1994.

_____. *The Jacob Engelbrecht Death Ledger of Frederick County, Maryland 1820-1890.* Monrovia, Md. Paw Prints, Inc. 1995.

_____. *The Jacob Engelbrecht Property and Almshouse Ledgers of Frederick County, Maryland.* Monrovia, Md. Paw Prints, Inc. 1996.

Ferrill, Matthew & Gilchrist, Robert. *Maryland Probate Records 1635-1777.* Volume 9.

Flowers, Susanne Files & Edith Olivia Eader. *The Frederick County, Maryland Will Index 1744-1946.* Monrovia, Md. Paw Prints, Inc. 1997

Frain, Elizabeth R. *Monocacy Cemetery, Beallsville, Montgomery County, Maryland.* Lovettsville, Va. 1997, Willow Bend Books.

Gaithersburg, Maryland, City. *Gaithersburg, The Heart of Montgomery County.* Privately printed. 1978

Gilland, Steve. *Frederick County Backgrounds.* Westminster, Maryland: Family Lines Publications, 1995.

_____. *Early Families of Frederick County, Maryland and Adams County, Pennsylvania.* Westminster, Maryland: Family Lines Publications, 1997.

Green, Karen Mauer. *The Maryland Gazette, Genealogical and Historical Abstracts, 1727-1761.* Galveston, TX The Frontier Press. 1989

Haney, Ritchie Lee. *1920 Census for Damascus, Montgomery County, Maryland.* From personal notes of his father, Ritchie E. Haney, census-taker. Damascus, Md. Private. 1997

Holdcraft, Jacob Mehrling. *Names in Stone; 75,000 Cemetery Inscriptions From Frederick County, Maryland.* Ann Arbor, Michigan. 1966. Reprinted with "More Names in Stone" in two volumes, Genealogical Publishing Co., Baltimore, 1985

Hopkins, G. M. *Atlas of Fifteen Miles Around Washington, Including the County of Montgomery, Maryland.* Baltimore, Md. Garamond/Pridemark Press, Inc. for the Montgomery County Historical Society. Original 1879. Reprint, 1975

Hurley, William Neal, Jr. *Our Maryland Heritage, Book One, The Fry Families.* Bowie, Md. Heritage Books, Inc. 1994

_____. *Our Maryland Heritage, Book Two, The Walker Families.* Bowie, Md. Heritage Books, Inc. 1997

_____. *Our Maryland Heritage, Book Three, The Fulks Families.* Bowie, Md. Heritage Books, Inc. 1997

_____. *Our Maryland Heritage, Book Four, The Watkins Families.* Bowie, Md. Heritage Books, Inc. 1997

_____. *Our Maryland Heritage, Book Five, The King Families.* Bowie, Md. Heritage Books, Inc. 1997

_____. *Our Maryland Heritage, Book Book Six, The Burdette Families.* Bowie, Md. Heritage Books, Inc. 1997

_____. *Our Maryland Heritage, Book Seven, The Soper Families.* Bowie, Md. Heritage Books, Inc. 1997

_____. *Our Maryland Heritage, Book Eight, The Brandenburg Families.* Bowie, Md. Heritage Books, Inc. 1997

_____. *Our Maryland Heritage, Book Nine, The Purdum Families.* Bowie, Md. Heritage Books, Inc. 1997

_____. *Our Maryland Heritage, Book Ten, The Perry Families.* Bowie, Md. Heritage Books, Inc. 1997

_____. *Our Maryland Heritage, Book Eleven, The Stottlemyer Families.* Bowie, Md. Heritage Books, Inc. 1997

_____. *Our Maryland Heritage, Book Twelve, The Browning Families.* Bowie, Md. Heritage Books, Inc. 1998

_____. *Our Maryland Heritage, Book Thirteen, The Miles Families.* Bowie, Md. Heritage Books, Inc. 1998

_____. *Our Maryland Heritage, Book Fourteen, The Lewis Families.* Bowie, Md. Heritage Books, Inc. 1998

_____. *Our Maryland Heritage, Book Fifteen, The Warfield Families.* Bowie, Md. Heritage Books, Inc. 1999

_____. *Our Maryland Heritage, Book Sixteen, The White Families.* Bowie, Md. Heritage Books, Inc. 1999

_____. *Our Maryland Heritage, Book Seventeen, The Mullinix Families.* Bowie, Md. Heritage Books, Inc. 1999

_____. *Our Maryland Heritage, Book Eighteen, The Young Families.* Bowie, Md. Heritage Books, Inc. 1999

_____. *Our Maryland Heritage, Book Nineteen, The Bowman and Gue Families.* Bowie, Md. Heritage Books, Inc. 1999

_____. *Our Maryland Heritage, Book Twenty, Trundle and Allied Families*. Bowie, Md. Heritage Books, Inc. 1999

_____. *Our Maryland Heritage, Book Twenty-one, Fisher and Beckwith Families*. Bowie, Md. Heritage Books, Inc. 1999

_____. *Our Maryland Heritage, Book Twenty-two, Davis Families*. Md. Heritage Books, Inc. 2000

_____. *Our Maryland Heritage, Book Twenty-three, Etchison Families*. Md. Heritage Books, Inc. 2000.

_____. *Our Maryland Heritage, Book Twenty-four, Holland Families*. Md. Heritage Books, Inc. 2000.

_____. *Our Maryland Heritage, Book Twenty-five, Ricketts Families*. Md. Heritage Books, Inc. 2000.

_____. *Our Maryland Heritage, Book Twenty-six, Trail Families*. Md. Heritage Books, Inc. 2000.

_____. *Our Maryland Heritage, Book Twenty-seven, Rabbitt Families*. Md. Heritage Books, Inc. 2000.

_____. *1850 Census of Montgomery County, Md*. Bowie, Md. Heritage Books, Inc. 1998

_____. *1860 Census of Montgomery County, Md*. Bowie, Md. Heritage Books, Inc. 1998

_____. *1870 Census of Montgomery County, Md*. Bowie, Md. Heritage Books, Inc. 1999

_____. *1880 Census of Montgomery County, Md*. Bowie, Md. Heritage Books, Inc. 1999

_____. *1900 Census of Montgomery County, Md*. Bowie, Md. Heritage Books, Inc. 2000

Malloy, Mary Gordon; Sween, Jane C.; Manuel, Janet D. *Abstract of Wills, Montgomery County, Maryland 1776-1825* Westminster, Md. Family Line Publications. 1989, 1998

Malloy, Mary Gordon; Jacobs, Marian W. *Genealogical Abstracts, Montgomery County Sentinel, 1855-1899*. Rockville, Md. Montgomery County Historical Society. 1986.

Manuel, Janet Thompson. *Montgomery County, Maryland Marriage Licenses, 1798-1898*. Westminster, Md. Family Line Publications. 1987, 1998

Maryland State. *Archives of Maryland*, all volumes.

Maryland Hall of Records. *Wills, estates, inventories, births, deaths, marriages, deeds and other reference works relative to counties of Maryland.*

_____. *Maryland Calendar of Wills.* All volumes.

_____. *Maryland Historical Society Magazine.*

_____. *Vestry Book of St. John's Episcopal Parish Church, 1689-1810.* Original.

Montgomery County Court Records. *Wills, inventories of estate, deeds.* Rockville, Maryland.

Montgomery County Historical Society, Rockville, Maryland. *Folder files; census, church, correspondence, newspaper, manuscripts, library, and family records.*

Myers, Margaret Elizabeth. *Marriage Licenses of Frederick County, Maryland 1778-1810.* Westminster, Md. Family Line Publications. Second Edition, 1994

_____. *Marriage Licenses of Frederick County, Maryland 1811-1840.* Family Line Publications. 1987

_____. *Marriage Licenses of Frederick County, Maryland 1841-1865.* Family Line Publications. 1988

Omans, Donald James and Nancy West. *Montgomery County (Maryland) Marriages 1798-1875.* Compiled by Potomack River Chapter, National Society of Colonial Dames. Athens, Georgia. 1987. Iberian Publishing Co.

Peden, Henry C., Jr. *Revolutionary Patriots of Prince George's County 1775-1783.* Westminster, Md. Family Line Publications. 1997

_____. *Revolutionary Patriots of Montgomery County 1776-1783.* Westminster, Md. Family Line Publications. 1996

Scharff, J. Thomas. *History of Maryland.* Three Volumes. Hatboro, Pennsylvania. Tradition Press. 1967

_____. *History of Western Maryland, Volume I.* Baltimore, Md. Genealogical Publishing Co., Inc. 1995

_____. *History of Western Maryland, Volume II.* Baltimore, Md. Genealogical Publishing Co., Inc. 1995

_____. *History of Western Maryland, Index to Volumes I and II.* By Helen Long (which see). Baltimore, Md. Genealogical Publishing Co., Inc. 1995

Tombstone Records. *Bethesda United Methodist Church, Browningsville, Maryland. Forest Oak Cemetery, Gaithersburg, Maryland. Goshen United Methodist Church (now Goshen Mennonite Church), Laytonsville, Maryland. St. Paul's Methodist Church, Laytonsville, Maryland.*

Williams, T. J. C. & Folger McKinsey. *History of Frederick County, Maryland, Volume 1.* Baltimore, Md. Genealogical Publishing Co., Inc. 1997

————. *History of Frederick County, Maryland, Volume 2.* Baltimore, Md. Genealogical Publishing Co., Inc. 1997

Wright, F. Edward.. *Marriages and Deaths in the Newspapers of Frederick and Montgomery Counties, Maryland. 1820-1830.* Westminster, Maryland: Family Lines Publications, 1992.

————. *Newspaper Abstracts of Frederick County 1811-1815.* Westminster, Md. Family Line Publications. 1992

————. *Newspaper Abstracts of Frederick County, 1816 to 1819.* Westminster, Maryland: Family Lines Publications, 1993.

————. *Frederick County Militia in the War of 1812.* Westminster, Md. Family Line Publications.

INDEX

All names appearing in the text have been indexed, with reference to each page on which they appear. Most names appear with a date, generally indicating date of birth, in order to differentiate between individuals having the same given name. In some cases where birth dates are not available, dates of marriage or death will appear, such as m/1825 or d/1876. In the case of common names such as John or Mary, where no date is specified, the references are without question to more than one individual.

Chiswell, Eleanor White 1822, 91
Chiswell, Eugenia Gott 1883, 92
Chiswell, John Augustus, III 1851, 92
Chiswell, John Augustus, Jr. 1830, 92
Chiswell, Joseph Newton 1812, 37
Chiswell, Lawrence Allnutt 1869, 50
Chiswell, Margaret White 1887, 93
Chiswell, Mary Collinson 1886, 92
Chiswell, Rebecca O'Dell, 84, 97
Chiswell, Sarah Constance 1906, 50
Chiswell, William Augustus 1783, 91
Chmieleweski, No given name, 55
Christner, Ida, 46
Cissel, Mariel Rebecca 1837, 87
Cissel, William 1803, 87
Clagett, H. Guiger, 76
Clagett, No given name, 5
Clare, Alexander A., 86
Clark, Carroll Gordon 1899, 42
Clark, Carroll Thomas 1923, 42
Clark, Hester Elizabeth 1902, 42
Clark, Otis G., 42
Clark, William Gordon 1918, 42
Clements, James Carroll, 94
Clements, Sarah Augusta 1863, 40
Clevinger, Norma Kay, 47
Clevinger, Norman, 47
Coates, Clarence J., 92
Cockey, Thomas, 70
Coffee, No given name, 57
Cole, Alice R. 1919, 32
Collinson, Edward, 82
Collinson, Mary Susanna, 88
Collinson, Sarah 1784, 82, 84, 87, 91,
    97, 111
Compton, Emily, 76
Conn, Margaret, 70
Connel, Mary A., 96
Connor, No given name, 80
Cool Spring Manor, 5, 6
Cooley, Charles Garrett, Jr., 104
Cooley, Charles Garrett, Sr. 1904,
    104
Cooley, Lawrence White, 104
Copp, Tracey Marie 1963, 44
Coughlan, John Fendall, 94

Coulter, Nora Miller, 38
Covington, Annie Laurie 1864, 88
Covington, Catherine Minerva, 85
Cramer, Mariam M. 1926, 109
Crandall, Esther, 73
Crandall, Francis, 73, 79
Crandall, Henry, 80
Crandall, Henry 1735, 79
Crandall, Henry Atwood, 79
Crandall, Richard, 80
Crane, George Washington, 84
Crane, Mary Catherine, 84
Crane, William C., 86
Crockett, Annie L. 1890, 27
Crockett, Bessie 1887, 27
Crockett, Edward E. 1860, 27
Cromwell, A. Hays 1877, 40
Cromwell, A. Hays 1905, 40
Cromwell, Anna Belle 1910, 40
Cromwell, Arthur 1837, 39
Cromwell, C. Mehrl 1901, 40
Cromwell, Carlton 1870, 40 -
Cromwell, Cleveland 1873, 40
Cromwell, E. Joanetts 1902, 40
Cromwell, Edna Clem 1875, 40
Cromwell, G. Elizabeth 1905, 41
Cromwell, J. Arthur 1903, 40
Cromwell, Nannie W. 1899, 40
Cromwell, Pearl 1903, 40
Cromwell, Richard 1880, 40
Crouch, Abigail F. 1844, 10
Crouch, Abraham 1801, 10
Crouch, Alfred 1833, 10
Crouch, John W. 1839, 10
Crouch, Mary E. 1841, 10
Crouch, Robert, 10
Crouch, Robert 1830, 10
Crouch, Sarah, 10
Crouch, Sarah E. 1835, 10
Crowther, Eleanor H., 22
Curren, Elizabeth 1823, 59
Curren, Jane, 59
Curren, William, 59

—D—

Daborne's Inheritance, 79
Dade, Alexander 1825, 99
Dade, Alonzo 1871, 100
Dade, Ernest 1856, 99
Dade, Joseph Townsend 1852, 99
Dade, Mary Jeanette 1853, 33
Dade, Mary Rebecca 1815, 33
Dade, Mary Ruth 1855, 99
Dade, Richard Gott 1853, 99
Dade, Robert, 114
Dade, Robert Townsend 1787, 99
Dade, Sallie, 100
Dade, Serena Elizabeth 1860, 100
Dade, Susan Ruth, 99
Dade, Thomas Collinson 1863, 100
Dade, Wade Hampton 1861, 100
Darby, Caleb, 84
Darby, Catherine Elizabeth, 103, 105
Darby, Genevieve Mattingly 1888, 50
Darby, George, 87
Darby, James Washington 1851, 33
Darby, John William, 36
Darby, Rebecca 1796, 84
Darby, Reginald James 1882, 33
Darby, Remus Riggs 1847, 50
Darby, Richard Edwin 1862, 36
Darby, Ruth Ellen 1902, 36
Darby, Susan Ellen 1831, 87
Darr, Mary Elizabeth, 43
Davis Leonard Isaac 1896, 22
Davis, Alan Clark 1960, 22
Davis, Amelia D. 1955, 22
Davis, Arundel Thomas 1847, 92
Davis, Carol 1928, 22
Davis, Charles Thomas 1952, 22
Davis, Clara Lena 1884, 19
Davis, Eleanor G. 1874, 92
Davis, Elma G. 1874, 91, 92
Davis, Emma A. 1873, 46
Davis, George Vernon 1857, 19
Davis, Harriet Jane 1921, 21
Davis, Ira Lynnwood, 19
Davis, Isaac, 4
Davis, Isaac Howard 1818, 19, 20

Davis, James Walter, 20
Davis, John Wallace 1854, 20, 52
Davis, John Wallace, III 1924, 22
Davis, John Wallace, IV 1950, 22
Davis, John Wallace, Jr. 1886, 21
Davis, Joshua 1803, 92
Davis, Laura Virginia 1914, 20, 52
Davis, Leona May 1885, 20
Davis, Leonard Isaac 1928, 22
Davis, Louise May 1885, 20
Davis, Louise Pearre 1886, 20, 51
Davis, Lynnwood 1916, 19
Davis, Margaret VanSise 1924, 22
Davis, Mary Catherine 1882, 19
Davis, Mary E., 15
Davis, Mary Loretta 1911, 20, 52
Davis, Mary Regina 1931, 23
Davis, Minnie Abigail, 22
Davis, Notley Hays, 20
Davis, Notley Hays 1883, 52
Davis, Notley Hays, Jr. 1919, 20, 52
Davis, Sherwin 1949, 19
Davis, Susan 1952, 19
Davis, T. Wallace, 51
Davis, Thomas Harold 1872, 92
Davis, Thomas Marshall 1905, 23
Davis, Thomas Marshall, Jr. 1925, 23
Davis, Timothy 1960, 19
Davis, Viola Estelle 1894, 22
Daw, Sarah Virginia, 7
Dawson, Eleanor, 82
Dawson, Virlinda Hawkins, 95
Dayhoff, Robert Thompson, 108
Deale, No given name, 80
Dean, Jean 1923, 38
Dean, Ralph H., 38
Deming, Eleanor Jeanette 1897, 38
Deming, Florella, 39
Deming, Florence 1895, 38
Deming, Frank C., 38
Dennis, Martha 1672, 1
Dennis, No given name, 60
Dent, Asa, 6
Dent, Robert, 6
Detrick, Kate H. 1925, 110
Devol, Brenton A. 1882, 53

—G—

Gaither, Zephaniah, 4
Galbreath, Isabelle, 86
Ganley, Gertrude H., 107
Garan, Al, 43
Gardiner's Addition, 1
Gardiner's Grove, 1
Gartrell, Sarah, 84
Gatewood, Ambrose, 117
Gatewood, Amy, 118
Gatewood, Elizabeth, 118
Gatewood, John, 117, 118
Gatewood, Joseph, 117
Gatewood, Mary, 118
Gatewood, Rachel, 118
Gatewood, Robert, 117
Gatewood, Sarah, 118
Gatewood, Thomas, 118
Gatewood, Thomas, Jr. 1710, 118
Gatewood, Thomas, Sr. 1687, 117
Gautres, Zephaniah, 4
Gaver, Mary 1799, 64
Geest, Christopher Clark, 42
Gill, Nellie Edna, 44
Girton, Clarissa W. 1825, 3
Glessner, Hannah, 10
Glessner, James, 10
Gloyd, Albert Leo 1941, 40
Gloyd, Clara Rebecca 1936, 40
Gloyd, James A. Hays 1931, 40
Gloyd, John Carroll 1925, 40
Gloyd, Joseph Cleveland 1932, 40
Gloyd, Mary Ann 1929, 40
Gloyd, Samuel Arthur 1865, 40
Gloyd, Samuel Arthur 1938, 40
Gloyd, Sarah Elizabeth 1927, 40
Gloyd, William Clements 1896, 40
Gloyd, William Cromwell 1924, 40
Gold, Elizabeth, 113
Gold, Inez, 113
Gold, John D. 1868, 113
Gold, Margaret B., 113
Goldsborough, 68
Gordon, Alexander, 67
Gordon, Elizabeth, 74

Gott's Hope, 71
Gott's Mill, 98
Gott, Achsah, 71
Gott, Alfred 1813, 71
Gott, Alice, 117
Gott, Ann, 70, 118
Gott, Ann Mary 1850, 92
Gott, Ann Virginia 1845, 114
Gott, Anna Dorothy 1899, 94
Gott, Anthony, 72, 79
Gott, Anthony 1694, 73, 79, 80
Gott, Anthony 1731, 71
Gott, Anthony, Jr., 79
Gott, Benjamin Collinson 1814, 84, 87
Gott, Benjamin Collinson 1866, 90
Gott, Benjamin Nathan 1856, 19, 56, 93
Gott, Benjamin Thomas 1885, 93
Gott, Capell 1709, 73
Gott, Caroline Eleanor 1884, 93
Gott, Cassandra 1728, 71
Gott, Claiborn 1808, 71
Gott, David 1815, 72
Gott, Dora Isabella 1860, 94
Gott, Dorothy Virginia 1903, 52, 89
Gott, Edward, 70
Gott, Edward Collinson 1809, 83
Gott, Edwin, 74, 76
Gott, Edwin Ezekiel 1824, 74, 76
Gott, Eleanor, 81
Gott, Eleanor 1760, 71
Gott, Eleanor 1811, 83
Gott, Eleanor 1819, 77
Gott, Eleanor M. 1893, 90
Gott, Eliza Jane 1823, 72
Gott, Elizabeth, 70, 80
Gott, Elizabeth 1724, 71
Gott, Elizabeth 1759, 71
Gott, Elizabeth 1781, 81, 94
Gott, Elizabeth 1798, 71
Gott, Elizabeth Ann 1798, 76
Gott, Elizabeth Ann 1810, 83, 88
Gott, Elizabeth Anne 1798, 74
Gott, Elizabeth Beall 1871, 90
Gott, Elizabeth L. 1897, 90

Hays, Eleanor Medora 1875, 32
Hays, Eliza 1809, 10
Hays, Elizabeth, 4, 5, 76
Hays, Elizabeth 1816, 7
Hays, Elizabeth 1828, 15
Hays, Elizabeth 1861, 59
Hays, Elizabeth A. 1826, 62
Hays, Elizabeth Eleanor 1818, 23, 35,
   36, 37, 38, 39, 41, 45, 47, 49, 52
Hays, Elizabeth Elliott, 58
Hays, Elizabeth Estep 1855, 15
Hays, Elizabeth m/1807, 8
Hays, Elizabeth Medora 1836, 30
Hays, Elizabeth Rawlings, 2
Hays, Elizabeth Ray, 31
Hays, Elizabeth Z. 1882, 32
Hays, Ellen, 63
Hays, Ellen 1820, 16
Hays, Eugene 1850, 14
Hays, Florence Elizabeth 1849, 17
Hays, Frances Eleanor 1846, 14
Hays, Franklin T. 1839, 25
Hays, Frederick Albert 1889, 32
Hays, Frederick Leonard 1885, 34
Hays, Frederick Poole 1846, 33
Hays, Frederick Poole, Jr. 1892, 34
Hays, Frederick Procorus 1846, 33
Hays, Frederick Sprigg 1893, 31
Hays, Frederick Sprigg, Jr. 1928, 31
Hays, George, 5
Hays, George Bussey 1752, 5, 6, 11
Hays, George H. 1802, 10
Hays, George H. 1829, 63
Hays, George R. 1827, 23
Hays, George W. 1838, 61
Hays, Georgiana 1850, 18
Hays, Goodlow 1817, 64
Hays, Harriet 1834, 60
Hays, Harriet Abigail 1830, 25
Hays, Harriet Abigail 1860, 20, 52
Hays, Harriet Levanda 1853, 18
Hays, Harrison 1841, 62
Hays, Harry W., 59
Hays, Hattie A. m/1877, 24
Hays, Helen S. 1923, 56
Hays, Henry C. 1838, 60

Hays, Hester, 4
Hays, Hink L. 1895, 32
Hays, Howard B. 1912, 56
Hays, Ira W. 1855, 65
Hays, J. Clyde, 65
Hays, Jahue, 57
Hays, Jake, 1
Hays, James, 1, 7
Hays, James 1831, 64
Hays, James C. 1876, 62
Hays, James T., 59
Hays, James Thomas 1833, 59
Hays, Jemima, 2
Hays, Jeremiah d/1783, 2, 4, 6
Hays, Jeremiah, Jr., 5
Hays, Jesse 1791, 4
Hays, John, 1, 2, 57, 58
Hays, John 1828, 60
Hays, John 1831, 59
Hays, John Coffee, General, 57
Hays, John H. T. 1813, 16, 19
Hays, John O. 1842, 12
Hays, John R., 9
Hays, John Ross, 59
Hays, John T. 1845, 17
Hays, John Thomas 1826, 59
Hays, John Witherow 1865, 59
Hays, Jonathan, 57
Hays, Jonathan, Jr., 57
Hays, Joseph, 58
Hays, Joseph 1781, 3
Hays, Joseph 1806, 61
Hays, Joseph 1828, 59
Hays, Joseph 1839, 61
Hays, Joseph L. 1883, 17, 19
Hays, Joseph, Jr., 58
Hays, Josephine H. 1834, 62
Hays, Josiah 1849, 64
Hays, Julia Ann 1794, 61
Hays, Julia Anne 1803, 60
Hays, Julian 1798, 61
Hays, Keturah 1799, 61
Hays, Laura J. 1843, 17
Hays, Laura Virginia 1859, 24
Hays, Lawrence Dade 1890, 34
Hays, Leo 1883, 17, 19

Hays, Leonard, 1
Hays, Leonard 1759, 11, 13, 15, 25, 28
Hays, Leonard 1889, Doctor, 30
Hays, Leonard Batson 1884, 32
Hays, Leonard Isaac Jones 1838, 30
Hays, Leonard John Odel 1842, 56
Hays, Leonard, Jr. 1793, 12, 28
Hays, Leroy, 65
Hays, Levi 1752, 3
Hays, Levi 1800, 10
Hays, Levi 1841, 3
Hays, Levin, 5
Hays, Levin 1803, 60
Hays, Lily Rawlings, 3
Hays, Linwood J., 93
Hays, Linwood J. m/1906, 56
Hays, Lizzie Ross, 60
Hays, Louisa E. 1871, 62
Hays, Lude 1877, 60
Hays, Lulah Mae 1930, 46
Hays, Lydia 1848, 60
Hays, M. R. 1825, 64
Hays, Margaret, 5
Hays, Maria L. 1838, 62
Hays, Maria Tillard 1842, 14
Hays, Mariah, 10
Hays, Mark A. 1881, 61
Hays, Martha, 3
Hays, Martha A. 1856, 56
Hays, Martha A. S. 1848, 60
Hays, Martha Jane, 7
Hays, Martha m/1804, 6
Hays, Martha Maria 1823, 15
Hays, Mary, 1, 2, 5, 8, 10, 58
Hays, Mary 1776, 64
Hays, Mary 1780, 62
Hays, Mary 1828, 15
Hays, Mary Alice 1850, 17, 18
Hays, Mary Ann 1793, 9
Hays, Mary Catherine 1843, 14
Hays, Mary Dade 1882, 33
Hays, Mary E. 1927, 56, 93
Hays, Mary Emma 1868, 24
Hays, Mary F., 4
Hays, Mary M. 1847, 64

Hays, Mary m/1801, 6
Hays, Mary Martha Poole 1849, 34
Hays, Mary Thomas 1853, 18
Hays, Mary White, 31
Hays, May 1849, 18
Hays, Melinda 1874, 62
Hays, Millie 1876, 32
Hays, Milton U. 1878, 60
Hays, Minnie 1873, 60
Hays, Nana P. 1880, 32
Hays, Nancy Ann W., 4
Hays, Nancy Mariah 1804, 10
Hays, Nathaniel d/1746, 2
Hays, Norris Harris 1784, 3
Hays, Notley 1760, 11
Hays, Notley 1762, 9, 16
Hays, Notley 1802, 10
Hays, Notley 1807, 10
Hays, Ola 1869, 60
Hays, Otho Thomas 1861, 24
Hays, Patience 1784, 9
Hays, Patricia Caywood, 46
Hays, Peter, 1
Hays, Priscilla, 5, 6
Hays, Priscilla Eleanor Elizabeth 1827, 28
Hays, Priscilla John 1835, 30
Hays, Rachel, 4
Hays, Rebecca, 4
Hays, Reverdy, 26
Hays, Reverdy 1782, 7
Hays, Reverdy William, 7
Hays, Richard, 5
Hays, Richard Estep 1837, 15
Hays, Richard Kenton 1886, 32
Hays, Richard Poole 1840, 31
Hays, Richard Poole 1877, 32
Hays, Richard Shirley 1891, 31
Hays, Robert Lee 1895, 32
Hays, Robert Townley 1887, 34
Hays, Rufus M., 65
Hays, Rutherford 1877, 60
Hays, S. A., 56
Hays, S. R., 56
Hays, Samuel, 1, 4
Hays, Samuel 1790, 3

139

Jones, Charles Robert 1918, 50
Jones, Charlotte Ann, 40
Jones, E. S. Mercer 1848, 51
Jones, Eleanor 1888, 34
Jones, Eleanor M., 19
Jones, Eleanor M. 1820, 16
Jones, Eliza M. 1879, 34
Jones, Elizabeth 1886, 34
Jones, Florence, 90
Jones, Henry Robert, 50
Jones, Joan Temple, 50
Jones, John 1839, 34
Jones, John Murray, 43
Jones, Joseph Luther, 86
Jones, Leonard Hays 1877, 34
Jones, Lloyd James 1878, 51
Jones, Lloyd James, Jr. 1911, 51
Jones, Lloyd S. 1808, 114
Jones, Margaret Virginia 1913, 50
Jones, Mary Alta 1869, 114
Jones, Mary C. 1876, 34
Jones, Mary Lucile 1880, 106
Jones, Mary Virginia 1906, 51
Jones, Pinkney 1882, 34
Jones, R. Elizabeth 1905, 51
Jones, Reginald 1895, 34
Jones, Reginald Bernard 1877, 50
Jones, Reginald Bernard 3rd, 50
Jones, Reginald Bernard, Jr. 1910, 50
Jones, Richard Lawrence, 50
Jones, Ruth Ellen W. 1838, 88
Justh, Elmer, 40
Justh, Helen Martin, 40
Justh, Joseph Elmer, 40
Justh, Mary Catherine 1933, 40
Justh, Robert Stanley, 40

—K—

Keiser, Mary Elizabeth, 91
Keller, Kathy 1943, 44
Keller, Patricia, 23
Kemp, Annie Kate, 47
Kessler, William Thomas, 50
Kibby, Joseph, 3
Kidwell, Martha Elizabeth, 43

King, Amber Nichole 1996, 45
King, David Andrew 1966, 45
King, Ernest Joseph, 75
King, Josiah Brandon 1996, 44
King, Krista Lyn 1984, 44
King, Leslie Crittenden 1896, 44
King, Leslie Lyn 1968, 45
King, Luther Roland, 108
King, Nannie A. 1905, 22
King, Paul Richard 1938, 44
King, Peter Brandon 1963, 44
Kirby, Barbara L. 1923, 110
Kirn, Andrew, 86
Kirn, Louise, 86
Kirn, Louise Alice, 86
Knott, Edward, 12
Knott, Joseph, 13
Knott, Lewis, 13
Knox, William, Captain, 58
Kraft, Daniel Leonard 1911, 43
Kraft, Mary Barbara 1936, 43
Kraft, Pamela Gay 1958, 43
Kraft, Sharon Ann 1953, 43
Kramer, Bertha Louella 1879, 39
Kramer, Blanch Deming 1897, 39
Kramer, Eleanor 1867, 38
Kramer, Emory H., 37
Kramer, Hester Trundle 1885, 53
Kramer, James, 52
Kramer, James Thomas 1902, 39
Kramer, James Thomas, Jr. 1933, 39
Kramer, Joanne Ellen 1929, 39
Kramer, John Frederick, 38
Kramer, John McAdams 1930, 39
Kramer, Lawrence Humphrey 1926, 39
Kramer, Ledru Rawlings 1872, 39
Kramer, Martha M., 38
Kramer, Martin Alvord 1932, 39
Kramer, Myrtle Marie, 37
Kramer, Ollie Leone, 37
Kramer, Samuel Brook Hayes, 38
Kramer, William Balster 1836, 38
Kramer, William Balster, 2nd 1870, 38

Kramer, William Balster, 3rd 1896, 39

Kramer, William Balster, 4th 1935, 39

Krebs, No given name, 22

—L—

Ladson, Herman Henry 1916, 108
Lakin, Alberta Trundle, 49
Lakin, Gerry, 49
Lamar, Benoni, 25
Lamar, Clarence H., 25
Lamar, John C. 1856, 24
Lambeth, Anne Roberts, 118
Lankford, William J., 99
Lawrence Eleanor T., 31
Leaman, Arthur, 12
Lee, Mildred Catherine, 35
Lee, Sarah Ann, 35
LeMaistre, Mary, 1, 2, 4, 5
LeMaistre, Richard 1670, 1
Lewis, Arthur Thomas 1864, 41
Lewis, Clyde Purnell 1893, 41
Lewis, Gertrude Estelle 1897, 41
Lewis, Mabelle Arthur 1900, 41
Liberty, 97
Linthicum, John Dutrow 1881, 20
Linthicum, Margaret Eleanor 1908, 105
Locust Neck, 68
Lok, No given name, 31
Long, Ada, 114
Long, Elijah White, 114
Long, Garland, 114
Long, Inez 1906, 114
Long, Isaac Trimble 1866, 114
Long, Isaac Trimble, Jr., 114
Luhn, Donald Delano, 104
Luhn, Dorothy White, 104
Luhn, Edgar Ray, 104
Luhn, Edgar Ray, Jr., 104
Lyons, Elizabeth L., 90

—M—

Magruder, Thomas F., 21
Magruder, Walter H., 21
Maple Lane, 20, 22
Martin, Brian Lee, 96
Martin, William C., 8
Mathews, Ellen F. 1842, 92
McAdams, Mary Ruth 1904, 39
McDermott, John 1860, 91
McElveen, Scott Elaine, 46
McGee, Blanche, 96
McIntosh, James, 117
McKechnie, Elizabeth, 8
McKinsey, No given name, 82
Meding, Harriet Barnes, 90
Mende, Blanche Veronica Marie, 109
Metcalf, Thomas, 73
Middlekauff, Mary V., 27
Miles, Catherine 1821, 19, 20
Miles, James Uriah 1821, 25
Millard, No given name, 56, 93
Miller, Julia Margaret, 101
Millspaugh, Daniel G., 81
Moler, Georgiana Lydia 1852, 45
Moler, Lucy Ione, 46
Moler, Miller P., 46
Moler, Philip Rion, 45
Montresor, 112
Moore, Agnes, 75
Moore, Barbara Collinson 1918, 108
Moore, Ethel Virginia, 108
Moore, Helen Boteler 1906, 108
Moore, James S. 1864, 107
Moore, John William, 108
Moore, John William, Jr. 1919, 109
Moore, Joseph Collinson 1910, 109
Moore, Mildred White 1904, 108
Moore, William Hempstone 1906, 109
Moran, Jane, 9
Morrison, Emily, 26
Mossburg, Charles, 96
Mossburg, Frank, 96
Mossburg, Ross, 96
Mount Carmel, 82, 98

143

—R—

Smith, Helen Leona, 48
Smith, Helen Lorraine, 48
Smith, Howard L., 48
Smith, Howard Travers, 48
Smith, Hugh Fairchild, 76
Smith, John, 58
Smith, Mary Ruth, 48
Smith, Mayme, 84
Smith, Virginia Howard 1902, 48
Smith, Walter Driscoll, 75
Smith, William, 117
Snively, E. D., 60
Snively, Isabelle, 60
Snively, Mary, 60
Snyder, Rebecca, 49
Soper, Alice Boteler 1911, 103
Soper, Cora W., 48
Soper, Daisy Collinson 1901, 103
Soper, Edna Grace 1895, 102
Soper, Eleanor m/1793, 73
Soper, Eleanor Stuart, 48
Soper, Elias Perry, 102
Soper, Elizabeth, 73
Soper, Harriet Elizabeth, 48
Soper, Henry Elias Perry 1868, 102
Soper, Howard Kent, 48
Soper, Leona White 1897, 103
Soper, Lingan Dow 1900, 103
Soper, Martha m/1801, 73
Soper, Nathan 1762, 73
Soper, Paul E., 48
Soper, Paul Mackley 1906, 103
Soper, Susanna Jackson m/1792, 73
Soper, Susannah Jackson, 73, 74
Spates, Frances Thomas, 42
Spates, Richard Thomas, 119
Specht, Abbie May, 106
Spencer, James, 81
Sprigg, Priscilla, 4, 5
Sprigg, Priscilla W., 28
St. Claire, Helen Esther 1907, 103
St. John, Thomas, 118
Stansbury, No given name, 70
Stansbury, Rachel, 70
Stansbury, Susanna, 70
Stepp, Howard, 41

Stepp, Louisjean 1934, 41
Stevens, Frances, 86
Stevens, Virginia, 85
Stinnett, Violet, 109
Stoakes, Florence, 8
Stoakes, No given name, 5
Stoney Castle, 111
Stottlemeyer, Joseph 1801, 64
Swann, Margaret E. 1935, 110
Swindell, No given name, 113
Swomley, Calvin Grant, 47
Swomley, Fannie Mae 1891, 47

—T—

Tabler, Ella Belle 1861, 19
Talbott, Henry W., 29
Talbott, Nathan T. 1819, 29
Taneyhill, Sarah 1834, 97
Tavener, Margaret T., 94
Tavenner, Clara, 40
Taylor, Lloyd Cecil, 44
Taylor, Lloyd Cecil, Jr. 1934, 44
Taylor, Sarah, 101
Taylor, Thomas, Colonel, 1
Tebbs, John Alexander, 113
Tebbs, Richard Henry, 113
Thackary, Christine Cora, 38
Thackary, Forrest Sidney, 38
The Fertile Plains, 80, 82, 87
Thomas, Bernard Hopkins 1912, 50
Thomas, Bernard O., 49
Thomas, Bernard O. 1882, 49
Thomas, Caroline Buckey, 48
Thomas, Charles Brosius 3rd 1935, 51
Thomas, Charles Purnell 1875, 42
Thomas, Charlotte Elizabeth 1876, 49
Thomas, Darius, 60
Thomas, David Dutrow 1845, 47
Thomas, David Dutrow 1871, 48
Thomas, David Dutrow, 3rd, 48
Thomas, David Dutrow, Jr., 48
Thomas, Edward O., 49
Thomas, Elizabeth, 48
Thomas, Elizabeth 1870, 42

Whitaker, Harriet Elizabeth 1857, 36
Whitaker, Theresa 1871, 37
Whitaker, Virginia Mildred 1866, 36
White, Albert 1855, 98
White, Albert Stephen 1902, 113
White, Alvin E. 1896, 101
White, Alvin H. 1927, 110
White, Alvin Hampton 1867, 101
White, Amy R. 1893, 101
White, Anna Marie 1939, 107
White, Anne, 114
White, Annie Laurie 1917, 89
White, Barbara Jane, 105
White, Benjamin 1752, 84, 97
White, Benjamin 1839, 85
White, Benjamin Edward 1880, 85
White, Benjamin Heath 1896, 113
White, Benjamin Lee 1877, 86
White, Benjamin M., 85
White, Benjamin S. 1828, 25
White, Benjamin Veirs 1865, 113
White, Betty Lee 1925, 110
White, Betty Warnetta 1911, 107
White, Carol Sue, 107
White, Catherine Bowman 1910, 105
White, Charles David, 105
White, Charles Ernest 1876, 106
White, Charles Ernest, Jr. 1913, 106
White, Charles LeRoy 1917, 110
White, Charles Stephen 1953, 110
White, Charles William, 84
White, Charlotte Marie 1947, 110
White, Cheryl Lynn 1944, 110
White, Dana L. 1959, 110
White, Donald Coplan 1915, 107
White, Dora, 85
White, Dorothy 1921, 89
White, Dorothy Elizabeth 1915, 110
White, Dougal, 85
White, E. Marie, 106
White, Edgar Gott 1871, 102
White, Edith Blanche 1899, 103
White, Edward C. 1868, 102
White, Edward Collinson 1832, 84
White, Edward Collinson, Jr., 85
White, Edward Oliver 1919, 89

White, Eleanor 1822, 37
White, Elijah Brockenborough 1862, 112
White, Elijah Brockenborough, II, 114
White, Elijah Veirs 1832, 111
White, Elijah Veirs 1899, 113
White, Elizabeth Beall 1920, 89
White, Elizabeth Virginia Sprecher 1882, 108
White, Estelle Elizabeth 1914, 105
White, George, 84
White, George William 1895, 85
White, Gerald LeRoy, 106
White, Gertrude Jeanette, 106
White, Grace Elizabeth 1905, 104
White, Harvey Jones 1869, 34
White, Hazelle 1888, 113
White, Helen B., 114
White, Helen Catherine 1904, 104
White, Helene Elaine 1946, 104
White, Henry 1858, 101
White, Henry Boteler 1870, 103
White, Hilleary Herndon 1859, 98
White, Ida 1871, 114
White, Inez Gott 1868, 113
White, Jane Elizabeth 1893, 113
White, John Collinson, 105
White, John Collinson 1833, 97, 102
White, John Collinson 1908, 106
White, John Collinson, Jr. 1867, 102
White, John Gott 1872, 114
White, John Grover 1886, 86
White, John Joseph, 104
White, Joseph Chiswell 1798, 97, 111
White, Joseph Collinson 1874, 106
White, Joseph Michael 1947, 109
White, Joseph Rodney 1914, 109
White, Joseph Rodney, Jr., 109
White, Joseph Thomas 1863, 101
White, Joseph Thomas 1865, 109
White, Joyce D. 1944, 109
White, Karla Kay 1946, 109
White, Katherine Elizabeth 1892, 34
White, Kathleen Dorothy 1910, 104
White, Laura Virginia 1868, 99
White, Lawrence Allnutt 1854, 89

White, Lillian Veirs 1893, 113
White, Lola, 84
White, Mabel Estella 1882, 86
White, Margaret Rebecca 1871, 85
White, Maria L. 1832, 12
White, Marjorie, 85
White, Martha, 75
White, Mary Ann 1843, 86
White, Mary Eleanor 1904, 105
White, Mary Eliza Waters 1867, 30
White, Mary Elizabeth 1875, 86
White, Mary Elizabeth Gott 1861, 112
White, Mary Estelle 1861, 101
White, Mary Margaret 1956, 110
White, Mary Priscilla 1868, 102
White, Mary Virginia, 85, 106
White, Mary W., 99
White, Maryanne, 105
White, Maurice 1875, 102
White, Melvin 1860, 112
White, Michael Specht 1909, 106
White, Mildred Susan 1878, 85
White, Nellie Boteler 1907, 104
White, Oliver Belt 1889, 89
White, Oliver Collinson 1878, 102
White, Raymond Elwood 1903, 103
White, Raymond Elwood, Jr., 104
White, Raynard Elwood 1903, 103
White, Richard 1856, 100
White, Richard Collinson, 85
White, Richard Eugene, 105
White, Richard Franklin, 86
White, Richard Gott 1826, 98
White, Richard Gott 1836, 85
White, Richard Gott 1870, 113
White, Richard Thomas 1829, 30
White, Robert Boteler 1939, 104
White, Robert William, 105
White, Roy 1879, 86
White, Samuel Benjamin 1796, 84
White, Sarah Ellen, 85
White, Sarah Ellen 1845, 87
White, Sarah Elsby 1880, 108
White, Sarah Griffith 1880, 119
White, Sarah Rebecca 1838, 109

White, Shirley, 107
White, Stephen Newton 1793, 112
White, Stephen Newton 1858, 112
White, Susan Ann, 85
White, Susan Ann 1828, 99
White, Susan Ann 1873, 86
White, Susan Ann 1878, 107
White, Susan Rebecca 1841, 86
White, Suzanne, 106
White, Thomas Earl, 101
White, Thomas Henry 1831, 100, 111, 115
White, Thomas Henry, Jr. 1895, 102, 115
White, Thomas Oliver 1862, 98
White, Wilford Lee 1940, 104
White, William Clyde, 85
White, William Earl 1920, 110
White, William Granville, 106
White, William Henry 1834, 85
White, William Lingin 1872, 104
White, William Lingin, Jr. 1916, 105
White, William Marshall 1908, 105
White, William Rodney 1890, 101, 109
White, William Rodney, III 1964, 110
White, William Rodney, Jr. 1930, 110
White, Willis 1859, 101
Wier, Martha, 75
Wiggins, Joseph St. Clair, 24
Wilburn, Mary, 2
Wilcox, George, 4
Wildman, Gladys, 87
Wilkerson, George, 4
Wilkey, Ann, 5
Williams, Elizabeth, 48
Williams, Lizzie B., 15
Williams, Margaret Mary 1922, 44
Williams, Nancy, 3
Williams, Nancy 1781, 4
Williams, Rachel Sarah 1812, 87
Williams, Richard W. 1815, 23
Williams, Robert McKendree 1904, 119
Williams, William McKendree 1875, 119

Willoughby, John, 68
Willson, Horace, Doctor, 15
Wilson, Albert 1840, 76
Wilson, Albert, Jr., 76
Wilson, Alvin Chesley 1836, 76
Wilson, Anne, 74, 76
Wilson, Eliel, 77
Wilson, Eliel Gott 1823, 75
Wilson, Eliel Soper 1829, 75
Wilson, Elizabeth Augusta 1892, 76
Wilson, Elizabeth Duvall 1849, 74
Wilson, Elizabeth Gott 1884, 76
Wilson, John, 74
Wilson, John Ezekiel 1825, 74
Wilson, John Fletcher, 74
Wilson, John Fletcher 1794, 76
Wilson, John Fletcher, II 1885, 76
Wilson, Julius Edwin 1834, 75
Wilson, Margaret Paret 1888, 76
Wilson, Mary Carr 1851, 75
Wilson, Samuel Augustus 1832, 75
Wilson, Sarah Eleanor 1886, 76
Wilson, Thomas, 58
Wilson, Thomas Oswald 1820, 75
Wilson, Virgil 1878, 76
Wilson, William H., 10
Wilson, William Wesley 1827, 75
Windsor, Benjamin, 87
Windsor, Edward William, 87

Windsor, Elsie Mae 1913, 96
Windsor, John Fleet, 87
Windsor, Joseph Edward 1880, 96
Windsor, Mary Susan, 87
Windsor, Reason Fletcher, 87
Wireman, Daniel 1790, 64
Wise, Mary Ann, 4
Wiseman, Sarah Louisa 1828, 10
Witherow, Sarah Ann 1832, 59
Wolf's Cow, 84, 97
Woodfield, Thomas, 69
Woods, No given name, 71
Woolen, John Sellman, 76

—Y—

Yeaman, Susan, 75
Yost, Alice Chiswell, 38
Yost, Howard B., 37
Yost, Roger Less, 38
Yost, Thomas Beidleman, 38
Young, Carrie Virginia, 89

—Z—

Zents, Dorothy, 48
Zimmerman, Marcel, 108